VISIT TO JAPAN

A TRAVEL GUIDE TO DISCOVER THE BEAUTY OF JAPAN

BECKY RHODES

INTRODUCTION

Maggie had always wanted to travel to Japan because of its fascinating culture, delectable cuisine, and breathtaking natural surroundings. She had been saving for this trip for years, and now that it was finally booked, she was eager to see everything that this amazing country had to offer.

In Tokyo, Maggie felt a mixture of excitement and trepidation as she got off the plane. She had never visited a nation where she couldn't communicate, so she wasn't sure how she would find her way about the city by herself.

Fortunately, she had done her homework and packed a dependable travel handbook to assist her in making plans for her trip. She had all the information she required to navigate the city in the guidebook, including thorough maps and bus schedules. It also included suggestions for the top local eateries and tourism destinations.

Maggie spent the following few days touring Tokyo's diverse areas, from the modern Akihabara neighborhood to the ancient Asakusa quarter. She experienced local cuisines like sushi and ramen, toured historic temples and shrines, and even participated in a traditional Japanese tea ceremony.

Maggie felt prepared and in control as she moved across the city thanks to her trip guides. She was able to stay away from the typical tourist traps and find hidden jewels that she otherwise would have missed.

Maggie continued to refer to her trusted travel guidebook, which gave her helpful insights into each destination, as she made her way from Tokyo to Kyoto and Osaka. She gained knowledge of each location's history and culture as well as useful details like available modes of transportation and regional traditions.

Maggie felt like a seasoned traveler by the time her vacation was over, certain that she could discover Japan on her own. She had experienced everything that the nation has to offer, from the frantic cities to the serene countryside. She was able to maximize her trip thanks in large part to her travel handbook.

Japan is a fascinating nation where old traditions and modernity coexist in perfect harmony. Japan offers a distinctive cultural experience that draws millions of tourists each year, from frantic cities to peaceful countryside. The country is a must-visit destination for tourists for a variety of reasons, including its distinctive architecture, delectable cuisine, exciting nightlife, and stunning natural surroundings.

Travelers to Japan should be aware of the country's customs and etiquette, which can be very different from your own. Making the most of your vacation will depend on your ability to recognize and respect the local culture. However, moving across the nation might be a snap if you are familiar with Japan's well-known for being reliable, and efficient transportation system.

Japan is more than just a popular tourist destination; it is a global cultural and technical powerhouse. The nation has a long, rich history, and its literature, music, and visual arts are well-known around the world. In addition, Japan is a leader in cutting-edge technology, including robotics and bullet trains.

Japan is a particularly distinctive tourism destination because of its diversity. Japan provides a wide variety of experiences to suit all tastes, from the neon-lit streets of Tokyo to the serene temples of Kyoto. Days can be spent taking in natural hot springs, strolling through crowded markets, or touring historic castles.

Japan is renowned for its warmth and courtesy, with a culture of decency and respect that permeates all facets of daily life. Travelers may anticipate receiving a warm welcome and being treated with the highest respect and courtesy in Japan, making it an inviting and safe destination.

In this Japanese travel guide, we'll examine some of the most popular cities there, like Tokyo, Kyoto, and Osaka, and give you advice on where to stay, what to eat, and what to see and do. This guide will provide you with all the details you need to organize a wonderful trip to Japan, whether your interests include visiting historic temples and shrines, indulging in the cuisine, or simply admiring the beauty of the country's natural surroundings.

CHAPTER ONE

WHY JAPAN IS A GREAT TRAVEL DESTINATION

Four major islands and numerous smaller ones make up the archipelago that is Japan. Anybody seeking a blend of culture, history, and modernity should consider visiting this distinctive nation in East Asia.

Japan is a fantastic tourist location for the following reasons:

1. Japan has a rich cultural and historical background, which can be seen in the many temples, shrines, and museums that it is home to. Tourists can explore historic temples including Kyoto's Fushimi Inari Taisha Shrine and Nara's Todai-ji Temple. The Tokyo National Museum, which boasts the greatest collection of art and archaeological relics in the nation, is one of the many top-notch museums in Japan.

2. **Delectable cuisine:** Sushi, ramen, tempura, and other mouthwatering dishes are all part of Japan's delectable cuisine, which is well known worldwide. Also, visitors can partake in sake tastings, traditional Japanese tea ceremonies, and cookery workshops where they can learn how to prepare Japanese cuisine.

3. **Unparalleled natural beauty:** Japan is home to breathtaking natural vistas, such as the recognizable Mount Fuji, national parks, and hot springs. Hiking, skiing, or simply taking in the landscape are all excellent ways for tourists to experience Japan's natural splendor.

4. **Advanced technology and innovation:** Japan is renowned for its innovative spirit, cutting-edge products, and one-of-a-kind devices. Guests can take advantage of unusual opportunities like vacationing in a robot hotel or visiting museums of cutting-edge technology.

5. **Bustling, vibrant cities**: Japan's cities are a perfect fusion of traditional and modern

culture. Tokyo, the nation's capital, is home to some of the most spectacular nightlife, shopping, and entertainment in the whole globe. A distinctive fusion of traditional architecture, cuisine, and culture can be found in other cities including Kyoto, Osaka, and Hiroshima.

6. **Generous people:** The Japanese are renowned for their friendliness and respect for foreigners. Communication between tourists and locals is simple because many Japanese individuals are English-speaking.

7. **Events and Festivals:** Japan is renowned for its vibrant and fun festivals that highlight the nation's rich culture and traditions. The well-known Cherry Blossom festival in the spring, the Gion Matsuri festival in Kyoto, and the Winter Festival in Sapporo are all events that tourists can take in.

8. **Transportation**: High-speed trains, buses, and subways are all part of one of the most effective and dependable transportation systems in the world, which is found in Japan. This makes it simple for tourists to

move about the nation and discover its many attractions.

9. **Secure and tidy:** Japan is renowned for its cleanliness and safety. The nation has a low crime rate, and its roads are kept in good condition. This makes it a fantastic destination for anybody looking for a secure and enjoyable trip, including families and lone visitors.

10. **Unusual Accommodations:** Japan has a variety of unusual lodging options, including capsule hotels, traditional ryokans, and contemporary luxury hotels. Guests can select from a variety of lodging options to fit their needs and budget.

11. **Shopping**: From high-end designer brands to reasonably priced and distinctive souvenirs, Japan is a shopper's paradise. Tourists can take pleasure in shopping in well-known districts like Tokyo's Shibuya and Ginza or Osaka's Shinsaibashi and Dotonbori.

12. **Pop Culture**: Japanese pop culture, which includes anime, manga, video games, and

fashion, is well-known worldwide. Visit specialized cafes, go to anime and manga events, or explore the different stores and arcades to get a taste of this dynamic pop culture scene.

Japan is a wonderful holiday location that has something to offer everyone, in conclusion. Japan is a must-visit location for anyone looking to have a unique travel experience because of its fascinating culture and history, delectable cuisine, stunning scenery, cutting-edge technology, amiable people, festivals, efficient transportation, safety, special accommodations, shopping, and pop culture.

BASIC INFORMATION ABOUT JAPAN (LOCATION, CLIMATE, LANGUAGE, CURRENCY, ETC.)

The East Asian island nation of Japan is located in the Pacific Ocean. It consists of a large number of smaller islands in addition to the four major islands of Honshu, Hokkaido, Kyushu, and Shikoku. Japan is situated north of China and Taiwan, east of the Korean Peninsula, and north of Russia.

A temperate climate with four distinct seasons can be found in Japan. Winters are cold and dry with considerable snowfall in some areas, while summers are hot and humid. The temperate and pleasant seasons of spring and autumn are when most people travel.

The majority of the population speaks Japanese, which is the official language of Japan. English is also commonly spoken, especially in big cities and popular tourist spots.

The Japanese Yen (JPY), which is widely acknowledged all around the nation, is the currency used in Japan. Moreover, credit cards are commonly accepted, especially in popular tourist locations and bigger cities.

Japan is well known for its extensive past, present, and traditions. It is a well-liked tourist attraction because of its distinctive fusion of cutting-edge technology and age-old customs. Tokyo, Mount Fuji, Kyoto, Hiroshima, and Osaka are a few of Japan's well-known tourist destinations. Sushi, ramen, and tempura are just a few of the delectable foods that are popular in Japan.

Here are some more details about Japan:

1. **Government and Politics:** Japan is a parliamentary constitutional monarchy where the Prime Minister leads the government and the Emperor serves as the ceremonial head of state. The Executive, Legislative, and Judicial branches of the Japanese government are separated.

2. **Population**: Over 126 million people were thought to reside in Japan as of 2021. The Greater Tokyo Area is the country's largest metropolitan area, and the majority of people reside there.

3. **Religion**: Buddhism and Shintoism, which have coexisted peacefully for millennia, are the two main religions practiced by the majority of people in Japan. In Japan, there are adherents of other religions as well as Christianity.

4. **Education**: Japan has a highly developed educational system and places a high priority on education. From elementary school through lower secondary school (ages 6–15),

education is required; high school is optional. Japan is known for emphasizing science and technology and has a large number of highly regarded universities.

Japan is a fascinating and distinctive nation with a long history, rich culture, and cutting-edge technology. It is a well-liked tourism destination and a genuinely special site to visit thanks to its distinctive fusion of classic and modern elements.

CHAPTER TWO

PLANNING YOUR TRIP TO JAPAN

It can be thrilling but sometimes overwhelming to plan a trip to Japan because there are so many incredible things to see and do there. There is something for everyone in Japan, whether you want to experience the busy metropolis streets of Tokyo or the serene beauty of Kyoto's historic temples.

The following advice can help you organize your trip:

1. **Choose your travel dates first:** Although you can visit Japan at any time of year, the best time to go depends on your interests and preferences. The best time to visit Japan if you want to see the renowned cherry blossoms is from late March to early April. Visit from mid-October to late November if you want to enjoy the milder temperatures and fall foliage. Avoid going during the Obon holiday (mid-August) and the Golden Week

holiday (late April to early May), as these are busy travel times.

2. **Establish your spending limit:** Japan can be expensive, but there are ways to cut costs. Set a budget for your travel, lodging, meals, and activities to get started. Consider purchasing discounted train and bus passes, and look into staying at hostels or Airbnb rentals for low-cost lodging.

3. **Purchase your tickets**: To get the best deals, purchase your tickets to Japan as soon as possible. There are various minor airports spread out around Japan, but the two main airports are Tokyo and Osaka.

4. **Obtain a tourist visa:** Before visiting Japan, you might be required to obtain a tourist visa, depending on your country of origin. For more information, contact the Japanese embassy or consulate in your country.

5. **Pick your lodging:** Japan offers a range of lodging options, from conventional ryokans to cutting-edge hotels. It is best to plan and

reserve your accommodations, especially during periods of high travel demand.

6. **Make an itinerary in advance:** There are a lot of sights and activities to take in while visiting Japan. Decide on the places and sites you wish to visit, and then look into your transportation alternatives. Make sure to provide enough time so you can appreciate each destination and account for any delays.

7. **Learn a few basic Japanese phrases to make your trip easier and more enjoyable:** Although many Japanese people are English speakers. Learn the words for "hello," "thank you," and "excuse me," as well as some frequent phrases for eating out and shopping.

8. **Take into account purchasing a Japan Rail Pass:** The Japan Rail Pass is an economical way to travel throughout the nation on JR trains and the Shinkansen (bullet train). The pass, which may be bought before you arrive in Japan, gives you unlimited travel privileges for a predetermined amount of time.

9. **Learn about regional customs and etiquette:** Visitors to Japan should be aware of the country's distinctive cultures many customs and etiquette conventions. For instance, it is appropriate to bow when introducing yourself to someone and to take off your shoes while entering a house or shrine. Conduct some homework in advance to prevent unintentionally offending residents.

10. **Sample the local cuisine:** From tempura and okonomiyaki to sushi and ramen, Japan is known for its delectable cuisine. Don't be scared to experiment and taste the regional cuisine. To sample a range of foods, think about going on a food tour or going to your neighborhood market.

11. **Pack appropriately:** You may need to bring different kinds of clothing and equipment depending on the season and your activities. Because so many sights take a lot of walking, be sure to carry good walking shoes. Be sure to wear clothing that covers your shoulders and knees if you intend to visit temples.

12. **Stay online**: You can access the internet while traveling by purchasing a SIM card for your phone or renting a pocket Wi-Fi. You'll be able to use menus and maps, as well as communicate with friends and family back home.

You may arrange a fantastic trip to Japan and take advantage of all that the nation has to offer by paying attention to these suggestions and doing some research beforehand. Japan is certain to make an impression, whether you're interested in its extensive history, stunning natural surroundings, or cutting-edge culture.

WHEN TO VISIT JAPAN

At any season of the year, it is worthwhile to travel to Japan because it is a stunning and diverse nation. The greatest time to visit Japan, however, will largely depend on your preferences and the things you wish to accomplish while there.

When arranging a trip to Japan, keep the following in mind:

1. **Weather**: There are four distinct seasons in Japan, and each has its distinct climate and landscape. One of the most popular seasons to travel to Japan is during the cherry blossom season, which lasts from March through May. Even though the summer months of June through August can be hot and muggy, it's a perfect time to visit Japan's many beaches and outdoor festivals. Winter (December to February) offers skiing and other winter sports in the northern regions, while fall (September to November) is famed for its stunning autumn foliage and comfortable temperatures.

2. **Crowds**: Because Japan is a well-liked tourist destination, there are times of the year when it gets busier than others. The busiest times in Japan are around the spring cherry blossom season and the winter vacation season around New Year's. Think about visiting Japan in the off-season to avoid the crowds.

3. **Festivals**: To commemorate the country's rich cultural heritage, there are numerous

festivals held all year long in Japan. Just two of the numerous festivals you may attend in Japan are the Gion Matsuri festival in Kyoto in July and the Nebuta Matsuri festival in Aomori in August.

4. **Budget**: Depending on the season, travel and lodging expenses in Japan can change. The low season (winter and summer) has the potential to be less expensive than the high season (spring and fall). But, keep in mind that during the off-season, some tourist sites can be closed.

5. **Cherry Blossom Season**: Because spring is cherry blossom season, it is the most popular time to travel to Japan. In the south, the cherry blossom season typically starts in late March and gradually extends up toward the north. Plan your trip for late March or early April if you want to experience the cherry blossoms in their full splendor.

6. **Golden Week:** In late April and early May, several national holidays are observed. At this time, a lot of Japanese people travel, and tourist destinations may be congested.

Yet, this can be a terrific time to visit if you're interested in learning about Japanese culture and festivals.

7. **Summer Festivals**: Many of Japan's well-known festivals, including the Gion Matsuri in Kyoto, Tenjin Matsuri in Osaka, and Awa Odori in Tokushima, take place during the summer. The culture and customs of Japan can be experienced through these festivals.

8. **Autumn Foliage**: If you want to see the stunning autumn foliage, fall is a fantastic time to visit Japan. In the northern regions, the change in leaf color often begins in late October and proceeds progressively southward. Kyoto, Nikko, and Hokkaido are well-known locations for autumnal foliage.

9. **Winter Sports:** If you enjoy winter sports, think about traveling to Japan in the winter. Excellent ski resorts in Japan include Hakuba in Nagano and Niseko in Hokkaido. Winter is a wonderful time to explore traditional Japanese culture, including onsen hot springs and holiday illuminations.

A year-round vacation destination, Japan has plenty to offer everyone. There are plenty of things to see and do in Japan, whether you're interested in cherry blossoms, festivals, autumnal foliage, or winter sports.

HOW TO GET TO JAPAN

Those who want to explore this intriguing nation may find that traveling to Japan is a thrilling experience. To travel to Japan, consider these options:

1. **By Plane**: Traveling to Japan by plane is the most popular and practical option. The busiest of Japan's international airports is Narita International Airport in Tokyo. Other significant airports in Japan include Haneda International Airport in Tokyo, Kansai International Airport in Osaka, and Chubu Centrair International Airport in Nagoya. Finding a convenient flight to Japan is simply because of the numerous major airlines that fly there from different places across the globe. Japan Airlines, ANA (All Nippon Airways), Delta, United, American,

Cathay Pacific, and Singapore Airlines are a few of the well-known airlines that offer flights to Japan.

2. **By Train:** Traveling to Japan by train is feasible if you are coming from a close-by nation like South Korea or China, but it is not recommended. Japan and its neighbors are connected by a small number of international rail services, such as the ferry train that runs from Busan, South Korea, to Fukuoka, Japan.

3. **By Cruise Ship:** Traveling to Japan by cruise ship is an additional option. Cruises to Japan are provided by several cruise lines, including Princess Cruises, Royal Caribbean, and Holland America Line. A cruise can be an excellent choice if you want to travel more leisurely and explore more of the area while getting to Japan.

4. **By Car**: Because Japan is an island nation, driving there is not an option. Yet, you can transport your vehicle on a ship from Russia or South Korea to Japan. Remember that

this can be an expensive choice and that most travelers might not find it useful.

Air travel is the most feasible and practical means of reaching Japan. Finding a flight that meets your demands and your budget is simple because there are so many airlines offering flights to Japan from different cities all over the world.

VISA REQUIREMENTS FOR JAPAN

Japan is a well-liked travel destination that draws tourists from all over the world. Before making travel plans, it's crucial to be aware of the visa requirements if you're thinking about visiting Japan.

An outline of Japan's visa requirements is provided below:

1. **Visa-free travel:** For stays of up to 90 days for tourism, business, or visiting friends and family, citizens of 68 nations—including the United States, Canada, Australia, and the majority of European nations—can enter Japan without a visa. To find out if you

qualify for visa-free travel, check with the Japanese embassy or consulate in your nation.

2. **Visa required:** Before traveling to Japan, you must obtain a visa if you are not a citizen of a nation that is exempt from visa requirements. You can apply for a visa for visiting family or friends, a business visa, or a tourist visa.

3. The application procedure varies depending on the nation from which you are requesting a Japanese visa. In general, you'll have to complete an application form and present a current passport, a recent photo, and records proving the reason for your travel, like hotel reservations or an invitation letter.

4. **Processing time for visas:** Depending on the nation from which you are applying, the processing time for a Japanese visa may differ. Applying for a visa can sometimes take several weeks, so it's best to do so well in advance of your intended trip.

5. **Duration of stay:** The duration of your stay in Japan is determined by the type of visa you are issued. Tourist visas normally permit stays of up to 90 days; however, business and visas for visits to family or friends may permit longer stays.

6. **Extension of stay**: You can request an extension of stay if you need to remain in Japan for a longer period than your visa permits. This procedure may be difficult and call for additional paperwork.

7. **Student visas**: A student visa is required if you intend to study in Japan. You must be enrolled in an approved educational program in Japan and have the money to sustain yourself while you are there to be eligible for a student visa.

8. **Working holiday visas:** If you are a young adult from a nation that has an agreement with Japan regarding working holidays, you may be qualified for a working holiday visa. You can travel and work in Japan for up to a year with this visa.

9. **Visas for cultural activities:** If you intend to engage in cultural activities in Japan, such as studying traditional Japanese arts or the language, you might be qualified for a visa for cultural activities. You must be sponsored by a legitimate Japanese organization to be granted this visa.

10. **Required paperwork:** You might be asked to submit additional paperwork to support your visa application in addition to the application form, passport, and photo. Depending on the type of visa you're applying for, this can contain a travel itinerary, evidence of financial assistance, and a certificate of eligibility.

Visa costs the cost of acquiring a Japanese visa varies depending on the kind of visa and the nation where the application is being made. When submitting your application, make sure to see the most recent pricing schedule.

In conclusion, there are various visas available for visiting Japan, each with specific needs and limitations. To guarantee a pleasant and trouble-free journey to Japan, be sure to confirm the precise visa requirements for your nation and make the necessary plans.

HOW TO GET AROUND JAPAN (TRANSPORTATION OPTIONS)

Japan has a robust and effective transportation system that makes traveling the entire nation simple and convenient. Travelers can choose from a variety of modes of transportation, including planes, buses, taxis, and rental automobiles. We shall thoroughly examine various transit options in this essay.

1. **Trains**: With over 27,000 kilometers of track and thousands of daily train services, Japan's railway system is one of the largest and most sophisticated in the world. The most widely used form of transportation in Japan is the train since it is hygienic, pleasant, on time, and swift.

   For travelers from outside Japan who want to travel by train throughout the nation, the Japan Rail Pass is a popular choice. For a predetermined number of days, it provides unlimited access to JR trains, including the Shinkansen (bullet train). The pass is a convenient way to travel across great distances and can be purchased before arriving in Japan.

Buses are a different, well-liked means of transportation in Japan, especially for short trips inside cities or between nearby towns. Local buses are affordable and simple to use, and bus stops always have detailed schedules and route maps accessible.

There are also long-distance buses with air conditioning, comfy seats, and restrooms accessible for intercity travel. These buses are a fantastic choice for travelers on a budget as they are typically less expensive than trains.

2. **Taxis**: With a distinctive sign on the roof and a light signaling availability, taxis are easily accessible in the majority of Japanese cities and villages.

Taxis are metered and their prices are higher than those of other forms of transportation, but they are a practical choice for short distances or when carrying a lot of goods.

3. **Rental Cars**: If you want to visit rural Japan or have more freedom with your itinerary, renting a car is a great choice. To rent a car in Japan, an international driving license is necessary. Rental car agencies have locations in important cities and airports.

   Driving in Japan can be difficult, especially in urban areas where parking can be difficult and expensive, and traffic can be high. Road signage and traffic regulations may also vary from those in other nations.

4. **Bicycle**: In Japan, especially in urban areas where traffic can be crowded, bicycles are a common form of transportation. Cycling is convenient and safe in many places because of its dedicated bicycle lanes. It's a cheap and convenient way to tour the towns and countryside of Japan to rent a bicycle.

5. **Ferries**: As an island nation, Japan frequently uses ferries to travel between its islands and coastal cities. In Japan, several ferry

companies run a variety of services, including passenger-only ferries and those that also transport cars and other vehicles.

Although it's important to keep in mind that ferry travel times can be longer than those of other means of transportation, it can be a beautiful and pleasant way to see Japan's beaches and outlying islands.

6. **Uber and other ride-sharing services:** Although these services are available in Japan, their use is not as widespread as it is in other nations. This is a result of stringent laws governing ride-sharing services that demand drivers to obtain particular licenses and restrict the kinds of vehicles that may be used.

Uber and other ride-sharing services can be pricey as a result, especially in locations where cabs are widely available. Yet, they can be a practical choice for those who must travel after hours when there are few public transit options.

In conclusion, there are many ways for visitors to discover Japan thanks to Japan's efficient and comprehensive transportation infrastructure. Each form of transportation has advantages and disadvantages, so picking the best one will rely on a number of variables, including your budget, schedule, and personal preferences.

CHAPTER THREE

TOP DESTINATIONS IN JAPAN

Millions of people visit the stunning and culturally diverse nation of Japan every year. It has a variety of locations, from traditional and tranquil rural landscapes to contemporary and futuristic metropolis. Following are a few of Japan's top travel destinations:

1. **Tokyo**: Every traveler should make a trip to Japan's capital city. It is a thriving metropolis with cutting-edge architecture, top-notch cuisine, and an exciting nightlife. The Imperial Palace, the Meiji Shrine, and the Tokyo National Museum are just a few of the historical and cultural sites in Tokyo.

2. **Kyoto**: Kyoto, the cultural epicenter of Japan, is a city rich in culture and tradition. There are more than 2,000 temples and shrines there, along with lovely gardens and old alleys. Attractions include the Arashiyama bamboo grove, Kiyomizu-Dera Temple, and Fushimi Inari Shrine.

3. **Osaka**: This vibrant city is well-known for its cuisine, nightlife, and shopping. There is a thriving street food scene there, and you must taste the takoyaki, which is well-known. One of Japan's most well-known theme parks, Universal Studios Japan, is also located in Osaka.

4. **Hokkaido**: The northernmost island in Japan, Hokkaido is renowned for its breathtaking natural beauty. Hot springs, ski resorts, and lovely national parks are all present. Hokkaido is a food lover's paradise because of its fame for seafood and dairy products.

5. **Hiroshima**: Despite its tragic past, the city of Hiroshima has emerged as a testament to resiliency and hope. To learn about the history of the city, you must visit the Peace Memorial Park and Museum. The Itsukushima Shrine and Miyajima Island are some other sights.

6. **Nara**: The small city of Nara is renowned for its deer park and historic temples. The largest bronze Buddha statue in the world

may be found at the Todaiji Temple, which is a UNESCO World Heritage Site. Also, the amiable deer that graze freely in the city's parks can be interacted with by visitors.

7. **Kanazawa**: This historic city is renowned for its beautiful gardens, art museums, and traditional Japanese architecture. The 21st Century Museum of Modern Art is a must-see for art enthusiasts, and the Kenrokuen Garden is regarded as one of Japan's most stunning gardens.

8. **Okinawa**: Situated in the far south of Japan, Okinawa is a collection of islands. Its stunning beaches, pristine waterways, and distinctive culture set it apart from the rest of Japan. The Churaumi Aquarium, one of the biggest aquariums in the world, is also located in Okinawa.

These are only a few of the most popular places in Japan. Japan is a country worth traveling to because each city and area has its distinctive charm and attractions.

TOKYO

The largest and most populated city in the world is Tokyo, which serves as the capital of Japan. With a population of more than 13 million, Tokyo is a thriving metropolis renowned for its distinctive fusion of traditional and modern culture.

The city is situated on the eastern coast of Honshu, the largest island in Japan, and is encircled by stunning mountain ranges. Tokyo's proximity to the Pacific Ocean has also had a big influence on its history and development. Due to its advantageous geographic position, the city has developed into one of Asia's most significant economic hubs.

Tokyo is a dynamic metropolis with a distinctive fusion of the old and new. Many historical sites can be found in the city, including the Tokyo Imperial Palace, which served as the home of Japan's emperors for more than a thousand years. The city is also home to numerous stunning temples and shrines that showcase Japan's diverse cultural heritage.

Tokyo is also renowned for its cutting-edge design, cutting-edge technology, and exciting nightlife. The city is home to several of the biggest tech companies in the world, making it a hotspot for fashion, entertainment, and technology. Tokyo is a well-liked location for both tourists and locals due to the abundance of hip restaurants, bars, and clubs there.

Exploring Tokyo's many neighborhoods, each with its distinct personality and allure is one of the finest ways to get a sense of the city. One of Tokyo's busiest and liveliest districts, Shinjuku is renowned for its tall skyscrapers, malls, and nightlife. Another well-known district is Shibuya, known for its lively streets, hip stores, and the well-known Shibuya Crossing.

Tokyo boasts a thriving food sector that is well-known worldwide. The city is home to a vast range of eateries and food markets that provide everything from international cuisine to traditional Japanese fares like sushi and ramen. The Tsukiji Fish Market, one of the biggest fish marketplaces in the world, is one of the greatest sites to explore Tokyo's culinary culture. The city's greatest sushi and the freshest seafood may be found here.

The numerous parks and gardens in Tokyo are a further well-liked destination. The Shinjuku Gyoen National Garden, one of the most well-known, is renowned for its breathtaking cherry blossoms in the spring. Yoyogi Park and the Meiji Jingu Shrine are some well-liked tourist attractions in the area.

Tokyo has a long history in popular culture, having given birth to numerous well-known anime and manga series. With a large number of stores and cafes devoted to anime and manga, the Akihabara neighborhood is regarded as the epicenter of the otaku culture.

Another district with a reputation for offbeat shops and street fashion in Harajuku. Despite its size, Tokyo boasts a strong public transit network that makes getting around the city simple. Tokyo's large metro network connects all areas of the city, making getting around the city simple. Tokyo is a good starting point for experiencing the rest of Japan because it is connected to other major cities by the Shinkansen bullet train.

Tokyo is a city that is rich in history and culture and also a center for cutting-edge technology and entertainment. It is a fascinating and distinctive location that has plenty to offer to everyone, from historic temples and customary festivals to cutting-edge technology and cutting-edge clothing.

KYOTO

On Japan's Honshu Island, in the center, is the city of Kyoto. It has a long cultural past and is famed for its geisha culture, traditional temples, shrines, and gardens. Before Tokyo took over as the nation's capital in 1868, Kyoto served as Japan's capital for more than a thousand years. It continues to be one of Japan's most culturally significant cities and draws millions of tourists each year from all over the world.

The Fushimi Inari Shrine, which honors Inari, the deity of rice and wealth, is among the most well-known sights in Kyoto. The temple is well-known for its countless vermilion torii gates, which form a passage through the woodland that resembles a tunnel. Tourists can stroll along the trail and take in the peaceful surroundings and stunning views of Kyoto.

The Kinkaku-ji Temple, popularly referred to as the Golden Pavilion, is another must-see sight in Kyoto. One of the most gorgeous locations in the city is a temple that is decorated in gold leaf and is situated next to a peaceful pond. Guests can stroll around the temple's gardens and marvel at the Golden Pavilion's magnificent reflections in the water.

The Gion neighborhood in Kyoto is a popular place to enjoy the ancient geisha culture. Visitors can observe geisha walking through the streets while dressed in traditional garb and get a look into their daily routines here. In one of the many teahouses in the region, visitors can also take part in a traditional tea ceremony or see a performance by a geisha and maiko (apprentice geisha).

Kyoto is renowned for its delectable cuisine as well. The most well-known meals include yudofu, a tofu-based hot pot dish, and kaiseki, a multi-course feast that emphasizes seasonal ingredients. Visitors can also try some of the region's sweets, like wagashi, which are mochi (a sticky rice cake) and sweet bean paste-based Japanese confections.

Several ancient temples and shrines may be found in Kyoto, including the well-known Kiyomizu-Dera Temple, which, from its elevated position, provides beautiful views of the city. The Ryoan-ji Temple's tranquil gardens, which include a well-known rock garden with 15 precisely placed stones, are also open to visitors. Nijo Castle, Ginkaku-ji Temple, and Sanjusangen-do Temple are a few other revered temples and shrines in Kyoto.

Arashiyama, a neighborhood on the outskirts of Kyoto, is another well-liked destination. Visitors can explore the well-known bamboo forest, take in the breathtaking scenery along the Hozu River, and pay a visit to the Tenryu-ji Temple, a UNESCO World Heritage site. In the neighborhood's Arashiyama Monkey Park, tourists may get up close and personal with Japanese macaques in their natural environment.

The traditional arts and crafts produced in Kyoto, such as textiles, lacquerware, and pottery, are also well-known. Visitors can buy these things from neighborhood shops or go to craft studios to observe the craftspeople at work. Visitors can discover the sophisticated weaving techniques utilized in the Nishijin district, which is well known for its textiles.

There are many museums and galleries to visit if one wants to learn more about Kyoto's history and culture. The Kyoto International Manga Museum is a must-see for fans of Japanese comics, while the Kyoto National Museum displays Japanese art and relics from many eras. The Kyoto Municipal Museum of Art, the Hosomi Museum, and the Museum of Kyoto are some of the other museums and galleries in Kyoto.

Kyoto not only has cultural attractions, but it's also a fantastic site to attend festivals and seasonal events. Several temples and parks offer breathtaking views of the pink blooms during the cherry blossom season in the spring, which is a popular time to visit. One of the most well-known festivals in Japan takes place in July and features street performances, parades, and traditional food stands.

All things considered, Kyoto is a city that offers a special fusion of antiquated customs and contemporary amenities. Tourists can explore the city's numerous cultural sites, take part in its authentic geisha culture, savor its delectable cuisine, and take in its breathtaking natural beauty. It's not surprising that Kyoto is still one of Japan's most popular tourist attractions.

OSAKA

In Japan's Kansai area, Osaka is a lively and bustling metropolis. The "Nation's Kitchen" and a popular culinary destination for both locals and visitors, Osaka is well-known for its food culture.

Dotonbori, a lively boulevard studded with neon lights, stores, and restaurants, is one of the most well-known parts of Osaka. The Glico Running Man and the Kani Doraku crab sign are two famous icons on the street. To enjoy regional foods like takoyaki, okonomiyaki, and kushikatsu, tourists visit Dotonbori.

Some of Japan's most well-known tourist destinations, including Osaka Castle, one of the nation's most recognizable landmarks, are also located in Osaka. The castle was built in the sixteenth century, and over the years it underwent numerous reconstructions. The park surrounding the castle is open for visitors to explore, and during cherry blossom season it is exceptionally lovely.

The theme park at Universal Studios Japan, which is on the outskirts of Osaka, is another well-liked destination. Together with its numerous rides and performances, the park is well-known for its Harry Potter theme.

In addition to its cuisine and tourist attractions, Osaka is a well-liked shopping city. Several shopping centers and areas, including Namba, Shinsaibashi, and Umeda, can be found in the city. Anything from high-end premium brands to reasonably priced mementos is available to visitors.

Osaka is an important business hub in Japan in addition to being a popular tourism destination. Osaka is the third-largest city in Japan, and more than 19 million people are living there. Electronics, pharmaceuticals, and textile industries, for instance, are major employers in the city.

The dialect of Osaka is one of its distinctive features. The "Osaka-ben" dialect of Osaka differs from standard Japanese in its vocabulary, intonation, and use of slang. Osaka is famed for its sense of humor and is the home of many comedians and entertainers in Japan.

The traditional performing arts in Osaka are another aspect of its rich culture. Rakugo storytelling, Bunraku Puppet Theater, and Kabuki theater are all performed in the city. Seeing performances allows visitors to learn about the culture and history that underpin these artistic disciplines.

The Hanshin Tigers and the Orix Buffaloes, two professional baseball teams, are located in Osaka. The Osaka Evessa and Cerezo Osaka are professional basketball and soccer teams, respectively, that play in the city.

Finally, Osaka has a colorful history that will appeal to history buffs. The city, which once served as Japan's capital, was a significant hub for trade and business during the Edo era. Tourists can explore historical places including the Sumiyoshi Taisha Shrine, one of Japan's oldest shrines, and the Osaka Museum of History.

Let's sum up by saying that Osaka is a vibrant, energetic city. It provides an exceptional fusion of cuisine, culture, entertainment, and history, making it a must-visit location in Japan.

HIROSHIMA

The city of Hiroshima, which is situated in western Japan, is best known for being the scene of the first atomic bomb assault in history. A total of 140,000 people died after an atomic bomb was detonated on the city by the American forces on August 6, 1945.

The "Little Boy" bomb, which was dropped from the B-29 bomber Enola Gay, detonated 600 meters or so above the city. The atomic bomb produced tremendous destruction, and the city was all but devastated.

Several people were buried under the debris as buildings were leveled. Radiation illness, serious burns, and other injuries were sustained by those who survived the original explosion. As soon as Japan submitted to the Allied forces following the Hiroshima bombing, the Second World War officially came to an end.

The city of Hiroshima is now committed to world peace and nuclear disarmament. The Hiroshima Peace Memorial Park, which was created to remember the atomic bomb victims, is located in the city. The Peace Memorial Museum, which is a part of the park, uses displays and memorabilia to explain the tale of the bombing and its effects. The only structure from the location of the bombing that is still surviving is the renowned Atomic Bomb Dome, which is located in the park.

A thriving city with a deep history and culture is Hiroshima as well. It has a large number of museums, temples, and shrines as well as a thriving culinary scene with regional specialties including okonomiyaki made in the style of Hiroshima and oysters. The city is renowned for its lovely parks and gardens, which include Shukkei-en Garden and Hiroshima Castle.

Hiroshima has developed into a popular travel destination for people traveling from all over the world to pay their respects to the atomic bomb victims and get knowledge about the catastrophic effects of nuclear war. Visitors can discover the city's history and culture through a variety of tours and activities, such as walking tours of the Atomic Bomb Dome and the Peace Memorial Plaza, as well as excursions to the Hiroshima Peace Memorial Museum and other significant historical sites.

Seeing and speaking with atomic bomb survivors, known as hibakusha in Japan, is among the most moving experiences for tourists in Hiroshima. These people, who were kids or teenagers when the bombing occurred, recount their tales of survival and the difficulties they encountered in the wake of the tragedy. These first-hand tales serve as a potent reminder of the terrible human cost of conflict and the necessity of making progress toward a nuclear-weapons-free future.

Hiroshima has survived the horrific events of August 6, 1945, and has become a symbol of optimism and fortitude in the face of tragedy. Due to its dedication to promoting peace and warning the world about the risks of nuclear weapons, the city has come to represent harmony and peace. Hiroshima offers tourists the chance to explore the city's unique culture and traditions while also learning about its turbulent past.

NARA

The Japanese city of Nara, which is noted for its ancient temples and shrines, stunning natural scenery, and rich cultural legacy, is situated in the Kansai area. Nara, which served as Japan's capital from 710 to 784, is sometimes referred to be the birthplace of Japanese culture and retains a significant place in the history of the nation.

The various UNESCO World Heritage Sites in Nara, notably the Todai-ji Temple, which has the largest bronze Buddha statue in the world, and the Kasuga-Taisha Shrine, which is well-known for the hundreds of stone lanterns that line its approach, are among the city's main draws. The historic temples of Horyu-ji and Yakushi-ji, both of which date back to the eighth century and are regarded as some of the world's oldest wooden structures, are also open to visitors.

In addition to its cultural and historical significance, Nara is home to stunning natural landscapes, such as Nara Park, where people may interact and feed wild deer. Together with these significant cultural landmarks, the park is also home to the Nara National Museum, Kofuku-ji Temple, and Isuien Garden.

Nara provides a wide range of traditional Japanese experiences, including tea ceremonies, kimono rentals, and calligraphy classes, in addition to its temples, shrines, and natural attractions. Among the city's numerous eateries and food stands, visitors may also enjoy regional specialties like a grilled eel, sake, and sticky rice cakes called mochi.

For anybody interested in Japanese culture, history, or the natural world, Nara is a must-visit location. Nara offers a singular and remarkable travel experience that is likely to make an impression on travelers with its historic temples and shrines, wild deer, and stunning surroundings.

HAKONE

The Japanese prefecture of Kanagawa contains the hilly area known as Hakone. It is a well-liked vacation spot with a picturesque view of Mount Fuji and is well-known for its hot springs, stunning scenery, and cultural activities.

The Hakone Shrine, which is situated on the banks of Lake Ashi, is one of the attractions of Hakone. Visitors can find tranquility and inspiration at this

Japanese temple, which honors the mountain goddess. One of the most popular tourist attractions in Japan is the Torii gate at the shrine's entrance.

The hot springs in Hakone are very well-known, and they are thought to have medicinal qualities. At Hakone, there are a lot of hot spring resorts where guests can unwind and soak in the natural mineral waters. The Hakone Yumoto Onsen, which has long been a favorite among tourists, is the most well-known of these resorts.

The Hakone Open-Air Museum, which showcases a variety of modern sculptures and art installations, is another well-liked Hakone destination. The museum provides guests with a one-of-a-kind, immersive experience while being located in a lovely park.

Hakone has a variety of hiking routes and picturesque hikes with breathtaking views of the mountains and lakes nearby for those who appreciate the outdoors. Another well-liked method of taking in Hakone's natural splendor is to ride the Hakone Ropeway, which offers breathtaking views of the Owakudani Valley.

Ultimately, Hakone is an essential stop for tourists visiting Japan. It offers a singular and fascinating experience that is certain to leave a lasting impression thanks to its natural beauty, cultural attractions, and hot springs.

MT. FUJI

On Japan's island of Honshu, there is a famous mountain called Mt. Fuji, often known as Fuji-san. At a height of 3,776.24 meters (12,389 ft), it is the highest mountain in Japan and a well-known representation of Japanese identity and culture.

Japan regards Mt. Fuji, an active stratovolcano that last erupted in 1707 or 1708, as a sacred mountain. Since ancient times, millions of tourists have traveled there for pilgrimages and sightseeing, climbing the peak each year.

The five lakes that encircle the mountain—Lake Kawaguchi, Lake Yamanaka, Lake Sai, Lake Shoji, and Lake Motosu—offer various vantage points for breathtaking views of Mt. Fuji. On a clear day, Mt. Fuji is also visible from Tokyo, and it frequently appears in Japanese literature, art, and poetry.

Both tourists and locals enjoy climbing Mount Fuji, which is open for climbing from early July until early September. The Yoshida Route, which is one of the mountain's four primary summit paths, is the busiest. Although climbing Mt. Fuji might be difficult due to the steep, rocky terrain, the stunning sights are well worth the effort.

Mt. Fuji, a significant natural and cultural landmark in Japan, has been listed as a UNESCO World Heritage site since 2013. The mountain has been a significant part of Japanese culture for many years and continues to inspire and astound people everywhere.

Mt. Fuji is more than just a mountain; it plays a significant role in Japanese culture and spirituality. With its breathtaking beauty and quiet presence, it has served as a source of inspiration for several painters, poets, and writers over the years. Together with Mount Tate and Mount Haku, the mountain is one of Japan's Three Holy Mountains.

Also connected to Shintoism, the native religion of Japan, Mt. Fuji is thought to be the home of the goddess Sengen, who is revered for her fertility and protection. The goddess has numerous shrines and temples on the mountain, and there are numerous festivals and rites held there throughout the year.

Mt. Fuji is a significant geological location in addition to its cultural and spiritual value because it is an active volcano with a long history of eruptions. To safeguard the security of tourists and local inhabitants, scientists and officials continuously monitor the peak.

Despite its widespread appeal, climbing Mt. Fuji can be risky, thus tourists are recommended to be well-prepared and must abide by safety precautions. Climbers are urged to pack the necessary supplies and equipment because the mountain can be quite chilly, windy, and unexpected.

Ultimately, Mt. Fuji is a monument to the strength and beauty of nature as well as a significant emblem of Japanese culture and identity. Anybody traveling to Japan must experience it, and the experience will stay with you forever.

OKINAWA

A collection of islands known as Okinawa can be found in southern Japan. It is well-known for its stunning beaches, illustrious culture, and distinctive cuisine. The rich history of Okinawa distinguishes it from the rest of Japan.

Formerly, Okinawa was a separate nation known as the Ryukyu Kingdom. It served as a focal point for commercial and cultural interactions between Southeast Asia, China, and Japan. In the years following World War Two, the United States had a significant impact on Okinawa as well. The island was managed by the United States until 1972 when it was handed over to Japan.

Okinawa is well known for having a high percentage of centenarians and a lengthy life expectancy. Their traditional diet, which is largely composed of veggies, tofu, and fish, is partially to blame for this. Karate, a distinctive martial art that emerged in the Ryukyu Kingdom, is also practiced in Okinawa.

The Churaumi Aquarium is among Okinawa's top tourist destinations. It is one of the biggest aquariums in the world and showcases a diverse range of marine life, including sea turtles, whale sharks, and manta rays. The Okinawa World theme park, Kokusai Dori, and Shurijo Castle are among additional well-liked tourist attractions.

Okinawa is renowned for having stunning beaches. The Emerald Beach, which has white sand beaches and crystal clear waters, is one of the most well-known beaches. Sunayama Beach, Miyakojima Island, and Kouri Island are a few other well-known beaches.

As a result of centuries of contact and exchange with different civilizations, Okinawa is a melting pot of cultures and traditions. This is demonstrated by the numerous annual celebrations and occasions including the Shisa Dance Festival, the Orion Beer Festival, and the Okinawa International Film Festival.

The shisha, a legendary animal that resembles a lion-dog, is one of Okinawa's most well-known icons. Shisa statues can be seen all across the island, from temples and shrines to the tops of buildings. They are thought to fend off evil spirits and shield buildings from harm.

Moreover, Okinawa is the source of numerous distinctive goods and crafts that are exclusive to Japan. They include traditional ceramics like Yachimun, Bingata fabrics, and Ryukyu glassware. Visitors can browse the numerous stores and markets where these goods are sold and even try their hand at producing them.

Another significant draw for tourists is the natural beauty of Okinawa. The island is home to beautiful coral reefs, lush woods, and waterways that are crystal pure. Tourists can explore the abundant aquatic life that makes Okinawa home by snorkeling, diving, or taking a glass-bottom boat excursion. The Okinawa rail and the Okinawa woodpecker are only two examples of uncommon and endangered species that can be found in the deep subtropical forest known as Yanbaru Forest.

Okinawa is a distinct and fascinating place with a rich history, culture, and natural beauty, in conclusion. It is a location where guests may take in the ocean's splendor, discover the region's distinctive food, and learn about the traditions of the Ryukyu Kingdom.

CHAPTER FOUR

THINGS TO DO IN JAPAN

With a rich cultural background, a vast choice of activities, and numerous attractions, Japan is a fascinating and diverse country. The following activities will undoubtedly make your trip to Japan memorable:

1. **Sample Cuisine**: From tempura and yakitori to sushi and ramen, Japan is known for its delectable cuisine. When you're there, sample a variety of foods, and don't be hesitant to check out the local street food scene.

2. **Participate in a Traditional Japanese Festival:** Japan has a long history of festivals, or "matsuri," that happens all year long. These celebrations are a wonderful way to learn about Japanese culture because they frequently feature parades, music, and traditional attire.

3. **Take a hot spring bath:** Natural hot springs, or "onsen," which are abundant in Japan are said to have health advantages. Enjoy the stunning scenery while unwinding in the warm, mineral-rich water.

4. **Travel to Hiroshima:** The tragic events of August 6, 1945, when the first atomic bomb was dropped on the city, are forever associated with Hiroshima. The Peace Memorial Park and Museum are located in Hiroshima, which is a thriving and sophisticated city.

5. **Visit Mount Fuji:** Mount Fuji is the tallest mountain in Japan and is revered as a sacred site. Take a hike up to the summit or just take in the breathtaking scenery nearby.

6. **See the Snow Monkeys:** A family of Japanese macaques known for their affinity for hot springs resides in the Jigokudani Monkey Park. Visit the park to watch these lively monkeys in action.

7. **Shop in Harajuku:** The Tokyo neighborhood of Harajuku is renowned for its vibrant and

outlandish fashion scene. Explore the numerous stores and boutiques, and perhaps even purchase a few unusual keepsakes.

8. **Take in the Cherry Blossoms:** Cherry blossoms, which typically bloom in late March or early April, are a famous feature of Japan. For a glimpse of the stunning pink and white flowers that are blooming, take a stroll around a park or garden.

9. **Attend a Tea Ceremony:** The Japanese tea ceremony is a long-standing custom that is practiced every day. Take part in a tea ceremony to learn about the significance and history of this significant cultural tradition.

10. **Discover the Gion District:** The traditional geisha homes, winding streets, and old-fashioned structures that make up Kyoto's Gion district are well-known. Explore the area on foot to take in the splendor and charm of traditional Japan.

11. **Take the Shinkansen:** Japan's high-speed bullet train is a marvel of contemporary engineering. Experience the quickness and effectiveness of Japan's transportation network by using the train.

12. Visit the Tokyo Skytree, the tallest building in Japan, for breathtaking views of the city. Visit the summit to take in the expansive views from the observation deck.

13. **Visit the Akihabara District**: Fans of anime, manga and video games flock to Tokyo's Akihabara neighborhood. Explore the numerous boutiques and eateries devoted to these pop cultural trends.

14. **Visit the Itsukushima Shrine**: Situated on the island of Miyajima, the Itsukushima Shrine is a UNESCO World Heritage site. The temple is well-known for its "floating" torii gate, which, during high tide, seems to float on the water.

15. **Take a Sumo Wrestling Lesson**: Sumo wrestling is the national sport of Japan, and

learning this ancient martial art can be a fascinating and fun experience.

16. Visit the Tsukiji Fish Market in Tokyo, which is the world's largest fish marketplace. Visit the market and eat some of the local fish and sushi while you're there.

17. **Visit the Himeji Castle:** One of Japan's most stunning castles, the Himeji Castle is a UNESCO World Heritage site. Discover the many rooms of the castle and take in the breathtaking views from the top.

EXPLORE JAPANESE CULTURE AND HISTORY (MUSEUMS, TEMPLES, SHRINES, GARDENS, FESTIVALS)

Japan is a country rich in culture and history. Japanese culture continues to attract people around the world in many ways, from its ancient traditions and customs to its contemporary way of life. Here are some of the most important historical and cultural locations in Japan that tourists should visit.

MUSEUMS

Japan has many top-notch museums that showcase the art, history, and culture of the nation. The Tokyo National Museum, which has a sizable collection of Japanese art and antiques, and the Kyoto National Museum, which has a sizable collection of traditional Japanese crafts, are two of the most well-known institutions.

Another significant museum that chronicles the World War II atomic bombing of Hiroshima is the Hiroshima Peace Memorial Museum. Visitors get a look into the misery of war and the value of peace through this poignant and instructive experience.

SHRINES AND TEMPLES

Japan has a strong religious tradition, and there are several temples and shrines worth visiting all around the nation. The Sensoji Temple in Tokyo, the oldest temple in the city and one of the most well-known tourist locations in Japan, is among the most well-known.

Another must-see location in Kyoto is the Fushimi Inari Shrine, which is famous for its magnificent vermilion torii gates that weave their way up the mountainside. The Shinto god Inari, who is regarded as bringing success and fortune, is the subject of the shrine.

GARDENS

Japanese gardens are renowned for their aesthetic appeal, practicality, and serenity. Visitors frequently describe them as a serene oasis amid a busy metropolis since they are made to be places for thought and contemplation.

The Kenrokuen Garden in Kanazawa, which is regarded as one of the three most beautiful gardens in the nation, is one of the most well-known gardens in Japan. The Kinkakuji Temple Garden in Kyoto, which has a lovely gold-leafed pavilion set against a backdrop of lush vegetation, is another gorgeous garden.

FESTIVALS

Japanese festivals are a vibrant and exuberant celebration of the nation's customs and culture. They are a wonderful opportunity to interact with and experience the atmosphere of the Japanese holiday season.

The Gion Matsuri in Kyoto, which takes place in July and is renowned for its ornate floats and traditional costumes, is one of the most well-known celebrations. The Sapporo Snow Festival, which takes place in February and showcases enormous snow sculptures and a bustling environment, is another well-known celebration.

The country's numerous museums, temples, shrines, gardens, and festivals should be explored by tourists to fully appreciate Japan's rich cultural heritage. Japan's culture and history are diverse and fascinating.

TRY JAPANESE CUISINE (SUSHI, RAMEN, TEMPURA, SAKE, TEA)

The precise balancing act of flavors, textures, and presentation is a hallmark of Japanese cuisine. It's worth trying the many dishes that make up this distinctive culinary legacy if you haven't already.

The most popular Japanese cuisine is probably sushi, which is made of vinegared rice topped with a variety of foods like fish, shellfish, veggies, and eggs. Sushi comes in a wide variety of forms, from the traditional nigiri (a little piece of fish on top of rice) to maki rolls (seaweed-wrapped rolls filled with rice and other ingredients). Wasabi, a hot, green seasoning, and soy sauce are frequently paired with sushi.

Ramen, a substantial noodle soup often cooked with a rich broth and topped with meat, an egg, vegetables, and other toppings, is another traditional Japanese dish. Pork, chicken, or fish can all be used to make broth, which is frequently seasoned with soy sauce, miso, or salt.

In the well-known Japanese cuisine of tempura, seafood, vegetables, or even ice cream are battered and deep-fried. The batter has a light and crunchy texture since it is produced from a combination of flour, egg, and ice-cold water. A dipping sauce composed of soy sauce, dashi (a sort of fish stock), and mirin is sometimes served with tempura (a sweet rice wine).

Traditional Japanese rice wine known as sake is frequently paired with meals. Its flavor can be anything from sweet to dry and is produced by fermenting rice and water. Depending on the variety and the season, sake is frequently served either warm or chilled.

Finally, tea is a necessary component of every Japanese meal. Green tea is particularly ingrained in Japanese society and is frequently consumed before or after meals. It is renowned for its cool flavor and a host of health advantages, including antioxidant and anti-inflammatory effects.

Choose a reputed Japanese restaurant or sushi bar in your region if you've never tasted Japanese food before. You might be surprised at how much you like these distinct and mouth-watering flavors.

EXPERIENCE JAPANESE ENTERTAINMENT (KARAOKE, ANIME, MANGA, THEME PARKS)

People from all over the world are fascinated by Japan's distinctive kinds of entertainment as well as its rich culture and history. In Japan, you can enjoy a wide variety of entertainment options, including karaoke, anime, manga, and theme parks.

Visitors to Japan should experience karaoke, which is a popular hobby there. Japan is home to numerous karaoke bars that are open to both locals and visitors. These establishments offer a private space where social gatherings of friends or family can belt out their favorite songs. Karaoke bars serve a wide range of patrons and have a huge selection of songs in several languages, including Japanese, English, and Korean.

Two of Japan's most well-known cultural exports are anime and manga, both of which have a devoted following all over the world. Action, romance, humor, and drama are just a few of the many genres that anime, an animated series, can have. The Japanese comic book style known as manga, on the other hand, is read from right to left. The same genres as anime are covered by manga, and some manga has been turned into anime series.

In Japan, there are many shops dedicated to serving the needs of fans of anime and manga. These shops offer a variety of goods, such as apparel, plush toys, and figurines. Fans can also go to Akihabara, a neighborhood in Tokyo renowned as the heart of the anime and manga scene. Many game shops, cosplay stores, and anime and manga stores can be found in the neighborhood.

In addition, Japan is home to some of the world's most thrilling theme parks, which provide one-of-a-kind experiences. With millions of visitors each year, Tokyo Disneyland and Universal Studios Japan are two of the most well-known theme parks in the nation. These theme parks provide a variety of activities, such as roller coasters, live performances, and interactive encounters based on famous films and television shows.

In summary, enjoying Japanese entertainment is a distinctive and thrilling experience that shouldn't be missed. Japan offers a wide variety of entertainment alternatives that are sure to enthrall tourists of all ages, from enjoying the thrill of theme parks to singing karaoke with friends to immersing oneself in the world of anime and manga.

OUTDOOR ACTIVITIES IN JAPAN (HIKING, SKIING, SNORKELING, ETC.)

Outdoor activities are a common way to discover the beauty of Japan, a country with a rich natural landscape. There are numerous thrilling outdoor activities to enjoy in Japan, such as mountain hiking, skiing in the winter, and seaside snorkeling.

In Japan, hikers of all skill levels can choose from a wide variety of trails and routes. One of the most well-liked hiking areas in Japan is the central Honshu region's Japanese Mountains. The hikes nearby provide breathtaking views of woods, alpine lakes, and snow-capped mountains. Hakone National Park, Mount Fuji, and the Kumano Kodo route are a few other well-liked trekking destinations.

Skiing is another well-liked outdoor sport in Japan, which is renowned for having top-notch ski resorts. The snowy season normally lasts from December to April, with January and February offering the finest conditions. One of the most well-known ski areas in Japan is the Niseko Ski Resort in Hokkaido, which offers a variety of runs and powder snow. Hakuba in Nagano, Nozawa Onsen in Niigata, and

Zao Onsen in Yamagata are a few further well-known ski areas.

In Japan, snorkeling is a well-liked summertime pastime. Some of the best snorkeling spots in Japan are found in the crystal-clear waters surrounding the Okinawa Islands. Tropical fish, sea turtles, and manta rays are just a few of the aquatic animals that may be found in the area's coral reefs. The Izu Islands and the Ogasawara Islands are two further popular snorkeling locations.

Cycling is another well-liked outdoor sport in Japan, and there are many beautiful routes to choose from. A well-known cycling path that crosses seven islands in the Seto Inland Sea and provides breathtaking views of the water and bridges is called the Shimanami Kaido. Another well-liked cycling path in Tokyo that features a beautiful trail alongside the Tamagawa River is the Tamagawa River Cycling Route.

Japan also provides chances for camping, kayaking, rock climbing, and other outdoor pursuits. Japan is a wonderful location for outdoor enthusiasts because of its stunning natural landscape.

CHAPTER FIVE

ACCOMMODATION IN JAPAN

Japan offers a wide variety of lodging options, from contemporary hotels and hostels to ryokans, or traditional Japanese-style inns. Japan is known for being a safe and clean nation, and this reputation is mirrored in the caliber of its lodging.

- In Japan, ryokans are a distinctive type of lodging that provides guests with a flavor of the country's traditional culture. These inns frequently have futon beds, tatami-matted rooms, and Japanese-style meals served in the rooms. Onsen, or hot spring pools, are a common amenity for travelers looking for leisure at several ryokans.

- There are several Western-style hotels in Japan, from opulent 5-star establishments to more reasonably priced lodgings. In Japan, there are a lot of hotels that provide excellent customer service and extras like on-site dining options, exercise centers, and laundry services.

- For tourists on a tight budget, hostels are a popular alternative that is widely dispersed throughout Japan. Most hostels provide dorm-style lodging, although some also provide individual rooms. Also, many hostels in Japan have common areas for socializing with other visitors, like kitchens and lounges.

- Guesthouses and vacation rentals are two types of alternative lodging that have grown in popularity in Japan recently. These choices can include access to a kitchen and living area, as well as a more individualized and local experience.

- The location and transit choices should be taken into account when selecting lodging in Japan. Staying near a train station or subway line can make it simple to explore the area since Japan has a robust and effective public transportation system. It's also advisable to make hotel reservations well in advance, particularly during busy travel times like the New Year's holiday and the cherry blossom season.

Generally, Japan provides a wide variety of lodging choices to accommodate all travel needs and price ranges. No matter if you opt for a contemporary hotel or a traditional ryokan, Japan's lodging options are of the highest caliber.

TYPES OF ACCOMMODATION IN JAPAN (HOTELS, RYOKANS, HOSTELS, ETC.)

Japan is a popular tourist destination because of its vibrant culture, stunning natural surroundings, and cutting-edge technology. Japan provides a wide variety of lodging options to meet the various needs and tastes of tourists.

Here are some examples of the different lodging options one can find in Japan:

1. **Hotels**: Hotels are arguably the most popular type of lodging in Japan, offering everything from low-cost alternatives to upscale luxury lodging. Hotels may be found in practically every Japanese city, and they provide a range of amenities like dining options, spa services, and onsen (hot spring) pools.

2. Ryokans, which are traditional Japanese inns and provide an authentic experience. They frequently have tatami-matted rooms, futon mattresses, and shared bathrooms. Kaiseki (multi-course) meals are also available at some ryokans, and you can take advantage of the warm hospitality of the staff.

3. **Capsule hotels:** This unusual form of lodging is especially well-liked by budget tourists or those who only need a place to stay for a short period. These hotels have tiny, capsule-shaped sleeping pods that are frequently stacked on top of one another as well as communal areas like lounges and restrooms.

4. **Hostels**: Backpackers and solo travelers seeking a cheap place to stay frequently choose hostels. Typically, they provide dormitory-style lodging with communal amenities including bathrooms and common areas. In certain hostels in Japan, private rooms are available.

5. **Minshuku**: While less formal and more affordable than ryokans, minshuku is a type of Japanese guesthouse. You can connect with the people and discover more about Japanese culture, and meals and facilities are frequently shared.

6. **Airbnb**: Travelers seeking a more secluded and individualized experience are using Airbnb more and more frequently in Japan. On the portal, you can rent out properties in any style, including traditional Japanese homes (machiyas) and apartments.

You will undoubtedly be able to locate lodging in Japan that meets your demands and budget, regardless of the type you select. Everyone has a choice, whether they wish to experience modern Japan or immerse themselves in traditional Japanese culture.

HOW TO BOOK ACCOMMODATION IN JAPAN

It's important to understand how to book accommodations properly because doing so in Japan can differ slightly from doing it in other nations. Following are the steps you take to make a reservation for lodging in Japan:

1. **Pick the appropriate lodging type:** There are many different kinds of lodging options in Japan, including hotels, ryokans (traditional Japanese inns), hostels, and guesthouses. You can select the one that best suits you based on your preferences and financial constraints.

2. **Select your budget:** It's important to establish a budget before you begin looking for accommodations because Japan can be expensive and lodging costs can vary greatly.

3. **Find lodging:** Using online reservation services like Booking.com, Agoda, or Expedia is the best way to find lodging in Japan. Moreover, you can use Japan travel-focused websites like Japanican or Rakuten Travel.

4. **Verify the location:** Despite Japan's robust transportation system, it is still crucial to confirm the lodging's location. It's advisable to get lodging in the city center or close to a

railway station if you want to be close to famous tourist sites.

5. **Read reviews:** Before making a reservation for lodging in Japan, check out the feedback left by previous visitors. You'll get a better notion of what to anticipate from the lodging from this.

6. **Inspect the room amenities:** Because some accommodations in Japan may have few amenities, it's important to know what is provided. As an illustration, certain low-cost hotels might not offer private restrooms.

7. **Make reservations in advance**: Japan is a popular tourist destination, and hotels can get booked up quickly, especially in the summer. To avoid disappointment, it is essential to make your hotel reservations as early as possible.

8. **Review the cancellation policy:** Be sure to review the cancellation policy before making a reservation. While some motels can have tight cancellation policies, others might not charge you anything.

9. **Pay attention to check-in times:** Some lodgings in Japan may have set check-in hours. Verify the check-in hours and schedule your arrival appropriately.

10. **Take the room's size into account:** Rooms in Japan may be smaller than you are accustomed to, so be sure to check the room's dimensions before making a reservation.

11. **Search for specials and discounts**: Some lodgings may provide specials or discounts if you make a reservation directly through their website or if you book a longer stay.

12. **Recognize the various room types:** In Japan, there may be different room types available, such as Western-style beds or traditional Japanese-style rooms with tatami mats. Before making a reservation, be sure to comprehend the various room types.

13. **Be aware of the language barrier:** It's important to have a translation app or basic Japanese language skills to communicate

since not all accommodations in Japan may have English-speaking staff.

14. **Take the season into account:** The cost of lodging in Japan can change depending on the season. The busiest seasons are often spring (cherry blossom season) and fall (fall foliage season), with winter being a potential bargain season.

15. **Take into account where you stay:** Japan offers a variety of interesting lodging options, such as a traditional ryokan in the countryside or a capsule hotel in the city. For a distinctive experience, think about lodgings based on location.

In conclusion, reserving lodging in Japan needs some preparation and investigation, but if you follow the appropriate procedures, you may locate the ideal lodging for your trip.

TIPS FOR STAYING IN JAPANESE-STYLE ACCOMMODATION (E.G. SLEEPING ON FUTONS)

There's a good chance you'll get to stay in a Japanese-style hotel at some point if you're planning a vacation to Japan. Tatami mat floors and futon mattresses are common features of these traditional lodgings, also known as ryokans or minshukus, which provide a distinctive cultural experience.

The following advice will help you get the most out of your stay in a Japanese-style hotel:

1. **Become familiar with the etiquette**: Before your visit, spend some time learning about Japanese etiquette, especially about taking off your shoes and bowing. In lodgings decorated in the Japanese manner, you'll probably be required to take off your shoes, wear slippers inside, and bow to your host or other guests as a symbol of respect.

2. Be ready to sleep on a futon mattress that is placed directly on the tatami floor if you are staying in Japanese-style accommodations. Although it could seem firmer than you're used to, it's all part of the experience. Normally, your host will set up the futon for you, but if you're staying longer than one

night, you could be asked to assist with the bedding.

3. **Be mindful of the tatami mats:** Avoid wearing shoes or going barefoot on tatami mats since they are constructed of fragile, woven rushes. Look for footwear made exclusively for walking on tatami floors when you enter your room. To prevent the mats from being damaged, you should also avoid dragging luggage or other heavy objects across the floor.

4. **Take advantage of the onsen (hot spring) experience:** Many lodgings designed in the Japanese style have their onsen, which is excellent for unwinding after a long day of sightseeing. Be warned that swimsuits are not permitted and that you will be expected to wash completely before using the onsen.

5. **Enjoy the traditional Japanese cuisine:** Kaiseki meals, which are composed of numerous small dishes of exquisitely presented and expertly prepared food, are frequently served at Japanese-style lodgings. Be open to trying new foods, and don't be

shy about asking your host for advice or an explanation of any dishes that you are unsure of.

6. **Request assistance if you need it:** Your host will be happy to assist you with anything you require, including reserving a restaurant or setting up transportation. If you have any inquiries, don't be reluctant to do so!

7. **Comply with the rules and traditions:** Japanese-style accommodations frequently have customs and rules that differ from your own. For instance, some ryokans impose curfews or noise limitations. Respecting your host and other guests requires that you abide by these rules.

8. **Pack the proper clothing:** You might need to pack particular clothing depending on the time of year and where you are staying. You might need warm clothing and snow boots, for instance, if you're staying in a mountainous area in the winter. Ask your host for advice if you're unsure about what to bring.

9. **Benefit from cultural activities:** Many lodgings with a Japanese flair provide cultural activities like tea ceremonies or flower arranging lessons. This might be a pleasant opportunity to meet other visitors and discover more about Japanese culture.

10. **Travel light:** Japanese-style lodgings frequently have little room for storage, so it's a good idea to travel light. Consider keeping some of your stuff at a train station locker or luggage storage facility if you want to stay more than one night.

11. **Don't be reluctant to request adjustments:** If you have particular requirements, such as a softer mattress or a different kind of pillow, don't be reluctant to ask your host. They will make every effort to meet your needs.

12. **Be considerate of other guests' privacy:** Japanese-style lodging frequently features communal areas like dining rooms and bathrooms. Be considerate of other visitors' privacy and make an effort to keep the volume down, especially during calm times.

Being housed in Japanese-style lodging might be a unique cultural experience. You'll have a lovely time if you become familiar with the manners and traditions, respect the tatami mats, and enjoy the traditional meals and baths.

CHAPTER SIX

PRACTICAL INFORMATION FOR TRAVELING IN JAPAN

Japan is a multicultural nation with an interesting history and delectable cuisine. It's a well-liked vacation spot for tourists from all over the world, and with good reason. But, if you've never been to Japan before, it can also be a little intimidating to arrange a trip there. Here are some useful advice and details you should be aware of before traveling to Japan to make it as easy and pleasurable as possible.

1. **Visa Requirements:** If you are a national of one of the numerous nations with which Japan has a visa exemption agreement, you are permitted to stay in Japan for up to 90 days without a visa. You must apply for a visa in advance if you are from a nation that does.

2. **Language**: Because not everyone in Japan speaks English and because Japanese is the official language, it's a good idea to learn

some fundamental phrases before you travel. People who speak English are more likely to be found in popular tourist places, although having a translation app on your phone can be useful.

3. **Money**: The yen is the unit of exchange in Japan. Currency exchange services are available at airports, as well as at banks and post offices across the nation. The majority of stores and restaurants also accept credit cards, but just in case, it's a good idea to have some cash on hand.

4. **Transportation**: Trains, buses, and subways are all part of Japan's first-rate public transportation network. Purchasing a Japan Rail Pass before you travel will provide you with the most flexibility and allow you to travel on most trains in Japan for a set price. You can also pay for trains, buses, and subways in large cities using a prepaid transportation card like Suica or Pasmo.

5. **Food**: Delicious Japanese dishes like tempura, ramen, and sushi are well-known worldwide. Finding food that satisfies your

needs can be a little more difficult if you have dietary limitations. Although there are increasingly more restaurants that offer vegetarian and vegan options, it's still a good idea to research them beforehand and bring a card or translation app to explain your dietary needs.

6. **Accommodation**: There are many different places to stay in Japan, including hotels, hostels, and ryokans, which are traditional Japanese inns. Hostels are a terrific choice if you're on a tight budget because you can frequently find both private rooms and dorms there. However, ryokans can be more expensive than other options. They are a distinctive and traditional way to experience Japanese culture.

7. **Etiquette**: It's crucial to respect regional traditions because Japan has a distinct culture and etiquette. As an illustration, it's polite to bow when introducing yourself to someone and to avoid eating or drinking while crossing the street. Also, it's polite to take off your shoes when visiting specific establishments like restaurants.

8. **Safety**: Violent crime is uncommon in Japan, which is a very safe nation. Yet, it's still crucial to practice fundamental safety measures, like watching out for your possessions in public places and avoiding walking alone at night.

9. **Weather**: There are four distinct seasons in Japan, and the climate varies from region to region. Winters can be chilly and snowy, while summers can be hot and muggy. Because of the cherry blossoms, spring is a popular time to go, but it can get crowded. The gorgeous autumn foliage makes fall a fantastic time to go.

10. **Wi-Fi**: Many locations in Japan, including airports, train stations, and some cafes and restaurants, provide free Wi-Fi. Yet, outside of popular tourist destinations, it can be more difficult to locate free Wi-Fi. If you need to keep connected while traveling, think about renting a portable Wi-Fi gadget or purchasing a local SIM card.

11. Type A and Type B outlets are used in Japan, which is different from those used in many other nations. You'll need a plug adapter to charge your electronics if you're coming from a nation with a different type of outlet.

12. Tipping is uncommon in Japan, in contrast to many other nations. In rare circumstances, leaving a tip can even be considered impolite. Instead, concentrate on treating people who offer you service with courtesy and respect.

13. **Cultural experiences:** Visiting temples and shrines, donning a kimono, or taking part in a tea ceremony are just a few of the many cultural experiences available in Japan. To truly immerse oneself in Japanese culture, think about including some cultural events in your agenda.

14. **Shopping**: From electronics and gadgets to traditional crafts and souvenirs, Japan is renowned for its distinctive and high-quality products. Popular shopping areas like Ginza

in Tokyo or Shinsaibashi in Osaka are great places to go if you want to go shopping.

15. **Arrange your trip in advance**: Japan can be hectic and crowded, especially during the busiest travel times. To minimize disappointment, it's a good idea to schedule things like transportation and lodging in advance. Moreover, you may need reservations for some well-known sights, so be sure to check before you travel.

Ultimately, visiting Japan may be a gratifying and unforgettable experience. You can make the most of your vacation and thoroughly immerse yourself in Japanese culture by paying attention to this useful advice and tips.

JAPANESE CUSTOMS AND ETIQUETTE

Visitors from other parts of the world might not be familiar with Japan's distinctive customs and etiquette due to its vast cultural past. Social harmony, respect for others, and attention to detail are characteristics that are highly valued in Japanese society, and these values are mirrored in how individuals interact with one another and in the mannerisms they follow. We'll look at some of the most important Japanese traditions and manners in this article

1. **Bowing**: Japanese etiquette places a high value on bowing, which is used to communicate respect, thanks, regret, and other emotions. A suitable head nod when meeting someone for the first time is one. To convey more formality or respect, bow more deeply. A deeper bow is frequently employed in professional contexts to express respect for senior coworkers or customers.

2. **Taking off shoes**: When entering Japanese home or other traditional structures like temples or shrines, it's customary to take your shoes off. For guests to wear indoors, slippers might be made available. Separate slippers are frequently made available to wear when using the restroom.

3. **Giving gifts**: In Japanese culture, sending gifts is a significant aspect of expressing appreciation or regret. It is customary to

give and receive gifts with both hands. The giver should always present the gift with both hands. If not instructed to do so, the present should not be unwrapped in front of the giver.

4. **Dining manners**: Before consuming food, it is customary to say "itadakimasu," which means "I receive this food," in Japan. "Gochisousama deshita" is a phrase used to thank the host or restaurant staff after dinner. Moreover, throwing away food or leaving it on one's plate is uncouth. Chopsticks shouldn't be left protruding from a dish of rice since this would look like incense at a funeral.

5. **Quietness and covert communication**: Speaking loudly or interrupting other people is frowned upon in Japan because stillness is frequently prized there. In some circumstances, it's preferable to communicate indirectly, and it could be required to interpret someone else's meaning from context. Observing nonverbal signs like body language and facial expressions is also crucial.

6. **Private space**: In Japan, people value their privacy greatly, thus it's best to refrain from touching someone without their consent. In congested areas like trains or subways, people frequently avoid making eye contact with one another and maintain a respectable distance.

7. **Reliability**: Being late is frowned upon in Japan because punctuality is so highly valued there. The optimal time to come in a few minutes early, and it's crucial to let people know if you're going to be late.

8. **Body art**: Tattoos are frequently connected to organized crime in Japan and can be interpreted as a symbol of disdain or defiance. Tattoos are often not permitted in traditional Japanese hot springs and public swimming pools.

In conclusion, the peculiar culture and values of Japan are reflected in the customs and etiquette of the country. Visitors to Japan can demonstrate respect for the nation's traditions and leave a good impression on the people they meet by adhering to certain customs and manners.

JAPANESE LANGUAGE BASICS

Almost 128 million people, mostly in Japan, speak Japanese as a first language. Due to its intricate writing system and grammatical structure, it is regarded as one of the hardest languages for English speakers to learn. Yet learning Japanese may also be incredibly beneficial because it can give you a deeper appreciation for Japanese culture and present you with new chances for employment, study, and travel.

Here are some fundamental Japanese language concepts to get you started:

1. Hiragana, Katakana, and Kanji, a combination of three writing systems, are used in Japanese. Syllabic letters called Hiragana and Katakana are used to write words for which there are no Kanji counterparts. Kanji are ideographic characters that were adapted from Chinese and stand for concepts, ideas, and objects.

For advanced Japanese studies, it's crucial to learn how to read and write Kanji.

2. **Pronunciation**: There are 14 consonants and 5 vowels in the Japanese language. In contrast to English, each syllable in Japanese is made up of a consonant and a vowel. With a few exceptions, the pronunciation is largely straightforward.

3. **Vocabulary**: The Japanese language has many English loanwords, including "コンピューター" (konpyu-ta) for computer and "ビール" (bi-ru) for beer. Also, the lexicon of Japanese is distinctive, with words like honorific and humble reflecting the hierarchical structure of Japanese society.

4. **Grammar**: The subject-object-verb sentence structure of Japanese grammar is distinctive. In other words, a sentence's subject comes first, then its object, and last its verb. Also, there are different verb tenses in Japanese, such as past, present, and future, as well as formal and casual speaking.

5. **Pronouns**: The pronouns in Japanese, such as "Watashi" (I), "anata" (You), and "kare," vary depending on formality and familiarity (he). Understanding how to use the right pronoun depending on the circumstance is crucial.

6. **Counting**: Depending on the object being counted, the Japanese have various counting systems. For instance, distinct terms are used to count humans, flat items, and long objects. It's crucial to become familiar with the proper counting method for each circumstance.

7. **Culture**: Japanese culture has a big impact on the language, so it's important to grasp its nuances when learning the language. For instance, the language of Japan uses honorific and modest terms to represent the high emphasis that Japanese culture places on courtesy and respect.

In conclusion, learning Japanese can be a difficult but worthwhile endeavor. You may learn the fundamentals of the language and comprehend

Japanese culture better with perseverance and practice.

TIPS FOR USING PUBLIC TRANSPORTATION IN JAPAN

Japan is renowned for its proficient and solid public transportation framework. Here are a few ways to involve public transportation in Japan:

1. **Buy a Suica or Pasmo card:** Suica and Pasmo are battery-powered shrewd cards that can be utilized on trains, transports, and metros all through Japan. They can be bought at train stations and odds and ends shops and are a helpful method for paying for your passage without purchasing individual tickets each time.

2. **Keep the guidelines**: While involving public transportation in Japan, make certain to observe the guidelines. For instance, don't eat or drink on trains or transports, and make certain to remain in assigned regions on stages and in vehicles.

3. **Know the timetable:** Ensure you know the timetable for the trains or transports you want to take. Trains in Japan are typically extremely dependable, so it's vital to show up at the station on time.

4. **Utilize the guides and signs:** Train and transport stations in Japan have guides and signs in both Japanese and English. These can be extremely useful in exploring the situation and tracking down the right train or transport.

5. **Be ready for busy times:** Busy time in Japan can be exceptionally packed, particularly on trains and metros. Be ready for groups and attempt to try not to go during top hours if conceivable.

6. **Be deferential**: Japanese culture puts a high value on regard and good manners. Make certain to be aware of different travelers and follow legitimate manners, like surrendering your seat to old or impaired travelers.

7. **Exploit exceptional limits**: Many train organizations offer extraordinary limits for sightseers, like the JR Pass. Make certain to check for these limits before buying your tickets.

8. **Utilize the baggage stockpiling**: If you have gear, many train and transport stations in Japan offer coin-worked storage spaces or gear stockpiling administrations. This can be a helpful method for putting away your gear while you investigate.

By and large, involving public transportation in Japan can be an extraordinary method for getting around and seeing the country. By following these tips, you can make your excursion smoother and more agreeable.

MONEY MATTERS IN JAPAN (CURRENCY, ATMS, TIPPING)

Cash matters in Japan can be mistaken by explorers who are curious about the nation's money and installment customs.

Here are some significant things to realize about cash in Japan:

1. **Money**: The authority money in Japan is the yen (JPY). One yen is separated into 100 sen, yet sen coins are not generally utilized in Japan. Banknotes come in divisions of 1,000 yen, 2,000 yen, 5,000 yen, and 10,000 yen. Coins come in divisions of 1 yen, 5 yen, 10 yen, 50 yen, 100 yen, and 500 yen.

2. **ATMs**: ATMs are broadly accessible in Japan; however, it's critical to realize that not all ATMs acknowledge unfamiliar cards. ATMs at odds-and-ends shops like 7-Eleven, Family Store, and Lawson normally acknowledge unfamiliar cards, however many bank ATMs don't. It's also significant that ATMs in Japan are normally not accessible every minute of every day, and many close early or are shut at the end of the week and on occasion. Assuming you're heading out to Japan, it's really smart to check with your bank to check whether they have associations with Japanese banks that permit you to pull out cash without bringing about high expenses.

3. **MasterCard's**: MasterCard's are generally acknowledged in Japan, particularly in bigger urban communities and traveler regions. Notwithstanding, a few more modest shops and cafés may just acknowledge cash, so it's smart to convey some yen with you consistently. While utilizing a Visa in Japan, you might be approached to show distinguishing proof (like an identification) to confirm your personality.

4. **Tipping**: Tipping isn't standard in that frame of mind, truth is told, it very well may be viewed as discourteous or annoying. The Japanese accept that great help ought not to be out of the ordinary as per normal procedure and that tipping infers that the assistance was not adequate regardless. If you have any desire to show appreciation for good help, a straightforward "Arigatou gozaimasu" (thank you kindly) will get the job done.

HEALTH AND SAFETY TIPS FOR TRAVELING IN JAPAN

Heading out to Japan can be an interesting and remunerating experience. The nation offers a rich social legacy, flavorful cooking, and a shocking regular landscape. Be that as it may, it means a lot to play it safe to guarantee your well-being and security during your excursion.

Here are a few hints to remember:

1. **Receive an immunization shot**: Make a point to counsel your PCP about essential inoculations before your outing. Japan is by and large a protected objective, yet it is consistently smart to play it safe against potential well-being gambles.

2. **Convey medicine**: On the off chance that you have a previous ailment, try to convey sufficient prescription to last your whole excursion. Likewise, keep a duplicate of your remedy and convey it to you consistently.

3. **Remain hydrated:** Japan can be very blistering and muggy, particularly throughout the late spring months. Try to drink a lot of water to remain hydrated and stay away from heat-related illnesses.

4. **Watch what you eat**: Japanese food is famous for its heavenly and changed contributions; however, it is critical to be cautious about what you eat. Try to keep away from crude or half-cooked meat, fish, and eggs, as they can cause foodborne ailments.

5. **Practice great cleanliness:** Japan is by and large an extremely perfect nation; however, it is critical to pursue great cleanliness routines to forestall the spread of microbes. Clean up regularly and convey hand sanitizer with you consistently.

6. **Be aware of catastrophic events:** Japan is inclined to tremors, storms, and other catastrophic events. Try to remain informed about any possible dangers and adhere to the directions of neighborhood experts in the event of a crisis.

7. **Be conscious of neighborhood customs:** Japan has an exceptional culture and it is critical to be deferential to nearby traditions and customs. Dress unassumingly, take off

your shoes while entering a home or sanctuary, and keep away from clear or problematic ways of behaving.

8. **Be wary while going across the road:** In Japan, vehicles drive on the left half of the street, which can be mistaken for voyagers from nations where vehicles drive on the right. Continuously look left and right before going across the road and utilize person-on-foot intersections.

By following these tips, you can partake in a protected and solid excursion to Japan. Make sure to continuously know about your environmental factors and to look for clinical consideration assuming you experience any medical problems during your excursion.

CHAPTER SEVEN

SHOPPING IN JAPAN

Shopping in Japan is a thrilling and one-of-a-kind encounter that can offer a brief look into the country's rich culture and customs. Japan is known for its top-notch items, creative innovation, and excellent client assistance. From conventional business sectors to current malls, Japan brings something to the table for everybody.

One of the most famous shopping locations in Japan is Tokyo's Ginza region, known for its upscale stores, retail chains, and extravagant brands. Ginza is home to leading stores of renowned Japanese style brands like Uniqlo, Muji, and Comme des Garçons, as well as global extravagance brands like Chanel, Dior, and Louis Vuitton. Guests can likewise appreciate very good quality eating and amusement choices nearby.

One more famous shopping objective in Tokyo is Shibuya, known for its in-vogue design stores, gadgets stores, and retail chains. Shibuya is especially famous among youngsters, with many shops spending significant time on road style and embellishments. Shibuya is likewise home to the renowned Shibuya Crossing, perhaps of the most active convergence on the planet.

For those searching for a more customary shopping experience, Japan's many business sectors offer a brief look into neighborhood life and culture. One of the most renowned business sectors is the Tsukiji Fish Market in Tokyo, known for its new fish and sushi. The market draws in a great many guests every day, and guests can watch sell-offs of fish and other fish. Other famous business sectors remember Nishiki Market for Kyoto, known for its nearby food and bites, and Nakamise Shopping Road in Tokyo, known for its customary trinkets and desserts.

Japanese retail chains are likewise worth a visit, with many contributions to a wide assortment of items and administrations. Retail chains like Mitsukoshi and Isetan in Tokyo are known for their uncommon client care, lavish atmosphere, and a wide determination of top-notch items. Guests can appreciate all that from style and beauty care products to food and home merchandise.

All in all, shopping in Japan offers a one-of-a-kind and energizing experience for guests. Whether you're keen on extravagance brands or conventional business sectors, Japan brings something to the table for everybody. With excellent client assistance and top-notch items,

Japan's shopping society is certainly worth encountering.

POPULAR SHOPPING DESTINATIONS IN JAPAN (E.G. GINZA, SHIBUYA, AKIHABARA)

Japanese shopping objections offer a mix of conventional and present-day shopping encounters that take special care of everybody's inclinations. Here are probably the most famous shopping objections in Japan:

1. **Ginza**: Situated in the core of Tokyo, Ginza is one of the most famous shopping regions on the planet. It is home to a portion of the world's most rich brands, including Chanel, Dior, and Louis Vuitton. Aside from top-of-the-line shopping, Ginza likewise offers customary Japanese stores, including cafés and kabuki theaters.

2. **Shibuya**: Shibuya is a popular shopping locale that is famous among youngsters. It is home to the incredibly popular Shibuya crossing, which is a must-visit for any vacationer. The region is known for its chic

shops, including retail chains, stores, and popular streetwear shops.

3. **Akihabara**: Akihabara, otherwise called Electric Town, is a shopping region in Tokyo that is popular for its gadgets and otaku culture. The region is home to many hardware shops, gaming stores, and anime stock shops. It is additionally home to housekeeper bistros, where servers wearing servant outfits serve food and beverages.

4. **Harajuku**: Harajuku is an energetic shopping locale in Tokyo that is known for its in-vogue shops and road style. A center for youngsters needs to put itself out there through design. The region is home to probably the most brilliant and one-of-a-kind shops, including Lolita-style stores, classic dress shops, and popular shops.

5. **Osaka Namba**: Osaka Namba is a clamoring shopping region in Osaka that offers a novel mix of customary and present-day shopping encounters. The region is known for its shopping arcades, road sellers, and customary Japanese shops. It is additionally

home to probably the most current shopping buildings, including the Namba Parks and the Shinsaibashi Shopping Arcade.

6. **Sapporo**: Sapporo is a city situated in the northernmost piece of Japan and is well known for its shopping objections. The city is home to probably the biggest shopping centers in Japan, including the Sapporo Production line, the Aurora Town, and the Heavenly Spot. The region likewise offers customary Japanese stores, including keepsake shops and food markets.

All in all, Japan offers an exceptional shopping experience that takes care of everybody's inclinations. From very good quality extravagance brands to conventional Japanese stores and energetic road design, Japan has everything. A visit to any of these famous shopping objections makes certain to pass on you with enduring recollections and a craving to get back to this astounding country.

TRADITIONAL JAPANESE SOUVENIRS AND GIFTS

Japan is known for its rich social legacy and extraordinary artistic expressions that have gone down through the ages. Subsequently, conventional Japanese keepsakes and gifts are profoundly pursued by explorers and authorities alike. From perplexing ceramics to wonderful materials, here are a few instances of conventional Japanese keepsakes and gifts.

1. **Earthenware Product:** Japan has a long practice of ceramic creation, with various locales of the nation known for their unmistakable styles. One famous sort of Japanese earthenware product is the Arita-yaki, which is known for its blue and white examples. Other well-known earthenware keepsakes incorporate Imari-yaki, Kutani-yaki, and Hagi-yaki.

2. **Furoshiki**: Furoshiki is a conventional Japanese wrapping material that can be utilized to wrap gifts or convey things. These fabrics arrive in different sizes and examples and are frequently adorned with lovely customary Japanese plans. Furoshiki fabrics are eco-accommodating, reusable, and make a one-of-a-kind and useful keepsake.

3. **Japanese Fans**: Japanese fans, or uchiwa, are famous trinket things that include lovely plans and multifaceted examples. They are frequently produced using bamboo and paper and arrive in a scope of sizes and styles. Uchiwa fans can be utilized to chill off on a hot day or shown as an enriching thing.

4. **Customary Dress**: Conventional Japanese attire, like kimono and yukata, make a wonderful and one-of-a-kind gift. These pieces of clothing arrive in different styles and varieties and can be worn for unique events or shown as enriching things. For the people who favor a more reasonable choice, tenugui (Japanese hand towels) make an incredible keepsake too.

5. **Japanese Desserts**: Japanese desserts, or wagashi, are a well-known gift that arrives in a scope of flavors and plans. These desserts are frequently made with conventional fixings, for example, mochi, sweet bean glue, and matcha powder. They make an incredible gift for those with a sweet tooth

and can be found at niche stores or retail chains.

6. **Japanese Writing material**: Japanese writing material is eminent for its excellent and remarkable plans. From washi tape to embellishing paper, there is an extensive variety of writing materials that make incredible trinkets. A few famous brands incorporate Midori, MT Covering Tape, and KOKUYO.

7. **Japanese Tea**: Japan is popular for its tea culture, and various sorts of Japanese tea make incredible trinkets. Green tea, for example, sencha or matcha, is a famous decision. Tea can be found in free-leaf structures or tea sacks and can be bought at specialty cafés or retail chains.

8. **Chopsticks**: Chopsticks, or hashi, are a fundamental piece of Japanese cooking. They arrive in various styles, from plain bamboo to unpredictably enhanced lacquerware. Chopsticks are functional and reasonable trinkets and cause an incredible

gift for individuals who appreciate Japanese food.

9. **Japanese Calligraphy:** Japanese calligraphy, or shodo, is a lovely and unpredictable work of art that has been polished in Japan for a long time. Calligraphy brushes, ink, and paper make extraordinary trinkets for those inspired by the work of art. For people who need a more interesting gift, a calligraphy look with a customized message can be dispatched.

10. **Maneki Neko:** Maneki Neko, or the "fortunate feline," is a famous Japanese doll that is said to bring the best of luck and fortune. These fired or plastic felines are many times found in retail facades or eateries, with their paw brought up in an inviting motion. They arrive in various sizes and plans and make a tomfoolery and one-of-a-kind gift.

All in all, conventional Japanese keepsakes and gifts offer a one-of-a-kind look into Japan's rich social legacy. Whether you are searching for a viable thing like a furoshiki or an improving thing like a kimono, there is a conventional Japanese keepsake that will suit your taste.

JAPANESE FASHION AND BEAUTY PRODUCTS

Japan has for quite some time been known for its remarkable design and excellent patterns, with an unmistakable style that is both moderate and cutting edge. Here are the absolute most famous Japanese style and magnificence items:

1. **Beauty care products:** Japanese excellent items are known for their excellent and imaginative fixings. Famous brands incorporate Shiseido, SK-II, and Kanebo. Japanese excellence items frequently center around accomplishing "mochi skin" or skin that is stout and young looking. This is accomplished using saturating fixings, for example, hyaluronic corrosive and collagen.

2. **Sheet Covers:** Sheet veils are a staple in Japanese excellence schedules. These covers are made of a slight sheet of texture or paper that is absorbed by serum and put over the face for 15-20 minutes. They are a

simple and viable method for providing your skin with an increase in hydration and other gainful fixings.

3. **Konjac Wipes:** Konjac wipes are a characteristic option in contrast to conventional face wipes. They are produced using the base of the konjac plant and are delicate on the skin. They can be utilized to purify and shed the skin, leaving it smooth and delicate.

4. **Japanese Denim:** Japanese denim is known for its excellent and toughness. Brands, for example, Momotaro Pants and Unadulterated Blue Japan are exceptionally pursued by denim devotees. Japanese denim is many times made utilizing customary methods, for example, selvage denim, which makes a particular edge on the texture.

5. **Streetwear**: Japanese streetwear is exceptionally persuasive in the style world. Brands, for example, A Washing Chimp and Comme des Garçons have acquired a worldwide following. Japanese streetwear frequently includes striking illustrations and

dynamic tones, with an accentuation on larger-than-average outlines.

6. **Conventional Attire**: Customary Japanese dresses like kimonos and yukata have become famous design things as of late. These pieces of clothing are frequently worn to formal occasions or as a feature of a cosplay outfit. They are produced using great materials and element mind-boggling plans.

7. **Geta**: Geta are conventional Japanese shoes made of wood with a textured strap. They are frequently worn with yukata or kimono and are a smart method for finishing a conventional Japanese outfit.

8. **Hair Care**: Japanese hair care items are known for their quality and viability. Brands, for example, Shiseido and Tsubaki are well known for their shampoos and conditioners. Japanese hair care items frequently center on reinforcing and supporting the hair, with fixings, for example, camellia oil and rice grain oil.

9. **Skincare Devices:** Japanese excellence schedules frequently incorporate the utilization of skincare instruments, for example, gua sha stones and facial rollers. These devices are utilized to rub the skin, increment the bloodstream, and decrease puffiness. They are a viable method for upgrading the advantages of skincare items.

10. **Kawaii Style:** Kawaii, which signifies "charming" in Japanese, is a famous style in Japan. It frequently includes pastel tones, cushioned textures, and charming creature themes. Brands, for example, Liz Lisa and Saintly Pretty spend significant time in kawaii style, which has acquired a chasing after the world.

11. **Green Tea:** Green tea is a staple in Japanese culture and is known for its medical advantages. It is likewise a well-known fixing in skincare items, as it contains cell reinforcements that assist to shield the skin from ecological harm.

12. **Onsen Skin health management**: Onsen, or natural aquifers, are a well-known objective

in Japan for their unwinding and remedial properties. Healthy skin items contain mineral-rich water from these natural aquifers, which are accepted to have benefits for the skin.

Generally, Japanese design and excellent items offer a remarkable mix of custom and development. From excellent beauty care products to customary dresses, there is something for everybody in the realm of Japanese design and magnificence.

CHAPTER EIGHT

NIGHTLIFE IN JAPAN

Japan is a country that is known for its exceptional and dynamic culture. One part of this culture that is especially well known is its nightlife scene. Whether you are searching for a laid-back bar, a top-of-the-line dance club, or a conventional izakaya, Japan brings something to the table for everybody.

One of the most famous regions for nightlife in Japan is Tokyo's Shinjuku locale. This region is home to a variety of bars and clubs, going from little, comfortable spots to enormous, excessive settings. One of the most well-known clubs in Shinjuku is the renowned Robot Café, where supporters can partake in a stunning execution highlighting robots, artists, and unrecorded music.

One more famous region for nightlife in Japan is Osaka's Dotonbori locale. This region is known for its dynamic environment and road food, making it a famous destination for people who need to encounter the city's nightlife while likewise enjoying nearby cooking. In Dotonbori, you can track down everything from customary izakayas to popular bars and clubs.

Notwithstanding these famous objections, there are likewise numerous different urban communities and locales all through Japan that offers remarkable and energizing nightlife encounters. For instance, Kyoto is known for its conventional tea houses and geisha exhibitions, while Hokkaido is home to various ski resorts that offer après-ski nightlife.

About nightlife in Japan, there are a couple of things to remember. To start with, numerous settings have clothing standards, so make certain to check early and dress properly. Second, it is critical to be conscious of Japanese culture and customs, especially while visiting customary settings like tea houses or izakayas. At long last, make certain to bring cash, as numerous more modest bars and clubs don't acknowledge charge cards.

Generally, Japan's nightlife scene is assorted and energizing, offering something for everybody. Whether you are searching for a wild evening out on the town or a more easygoing night with companions, you make certain to track it down in Japan.

POPULAR NIGHTLIFE AREAS IN JAPAN (E.G. SHINJUKU, ROPPONGI, SHIBUYA)

Japan is known for its energetic and various nightlife, with various regions taking care of various preferences and inclinations. Here are probably the most famous nightlife regions in Japan:

1. **Shinjuku**: Situated in the core of Tokyo, Shinjuku is one of the most active nightlife regions in Japan. It is known for its neon-lit roads, various bars, clubs, and amusement settings. Kabukicho, a sub-locale of Shinjuku, is especially popular for its grown-up diversion foundations.

2. **Roppongi**: Situated in the Minato ward of Tokyo, Roppongi is one more famous nightlife regions in Japan. It is known for its upscale clubs, bars, and eateries taking care of the two local people and outsiders.

Roppongi Slopes and Tokyo Midtown are two of the biggest shopping and diversion buildings nearby.

3. **Shibuya**: Another clamoring nightlife area in Tokyo is Shibuya. This region is renowned for its enormous passerby crossing, known as the Shibuya Scramble Crossing. Shibuya is home to many clubs, bars, and unrecorded music scenes, taking care of a more youthful group.

4. **Osaka Namba**: Situated in Osaka, Namba is a clamoring diversion region known for its nightlife. The region has numerous theaters, films, and music scenes, as well as various bars and clubs. Dotonbori is a popular road in Namba, known for its neon signs and road food.

5. **Sapporo Susukino:** Situated in Sapporo, the biggest city on the island of Hokkaido, Susukino is known for its energetic nightlife. The region has many bars, clubs, and karaoke foundations, taking care of a more youthful group. Susukino is likewise well

known for its ramen eateries and fish markets.

6. **Fukuoka Nakasu**: Situated in Fukuoka, Nakasu is a famous nightlife region known for its lively climate. The region has many bars and clubs, as well as cafés and road food sellers. Nakasu is likewise home to the Fukuoka Yatai, an assortment of food slows down serving nearby fortes.

Generally speaking, Japan offers a different and energizing nightlife scene, with something for everybody. From the neon-lit roads of Shinjuku to the enthusiastic climate of Nakasu, there is no lack of choices for those hoping to investigate Japan's nightlife.

JAPANESE BARS AND CLUBS

In Japan, bars and clubs are a significant part of the country's public activity. They are spots where individuals assemble after work to loosen up, mingle, and live it up. There are different kinds of bars and clubs in Japan, each with its special climate and culture.

One of the most famous sorts of bars in Japan is the izakaya, which is a customary Japanese bar. Izakayas serve different dishes, for example, yakitori (barbecued chicken sticks), edamame (soybeans), and sashimi (crude fish). They likewise serve cocktails like purpose, shochu (a refined refreshment), and brew. Izakayas are known for their relaxed and easygoing environment, making them an incredible spot to spend time with companions.

One more well-known sort of bar in Japan is the karaoke bar. Karaoke bars are spots where individuals can sing their hearts out while appreciating drinks with companions. These bars frequently have private rooms that clients can lease to sing with their gathering without being upset by different benefactors. Karaoke bars are exceptionally famous in Japan and are many times open until late around evening time.

For the people who need to move the night away, there are clubs in Japan that take special care of different music sorts like techno, hip-bounce, and J-pop. The club scene in Japan is energetic, and many clubs have best-in-class sound frameworks and lighting. A few clubs even have live exhibitions by DJs and craftsmen, making them an extraordinary spot to encounter Japan's nightlife.

Japanese bars and clubs must frequently have severe clothing standards and entry strategies. A few clubs might require an enrollment or a booking before section, while others may just permit visitors who are over a particular age. It's dependably really smart to check the club's site or online entertainment pages for particular necessities before taking off.

Generally, Japanese bars and clubs are a fundamental piece of the nation's way of life and public activity. Whether you're hoping to loosen up over beverages and bites or dance the night away, there's something for everybody in Japan's bar and club scene.

NIGHTTIME ENTERTAINMENT OPTIONS IN JAPAN (E.G. KARAOKE, LIVE MUSIC, THEATER)

Japan is a country that genuinely wakes up around evening time, and there is no deficiency of diversion choices for those hoping to encounter the city in the evening. From the neon-lit roads of

Tokyo to the clamoring nightlife of Osaka, Japan offers an extensive variety of evening diversion choices to suit all preferences and spending plans.

KARAOKE

Karaoke is a quintessential Japanese hobby and one of the most famous evening diversion choices in the country. Numerous karaoke bars in Japan are open day in and day out and offer confidential spaces for gatherings of companions to sing their hearts out. Some karaoke bars additionally offer food and drink choices, making it the ideal spot to go through a whole night.

UNRECORDED MUSIC

Japan has a flourishing unrecorded music scene, with settings of all sizes facilitating shows over time. Tokyo's Shibuya and Shinjuku regions are known for their enthusiastic unrecorded music scenes, with famous settings like Liquidroom, Club Quattro, and The Wall facilitating both neighborhood and global demonstrations.

THEATER

Japan has a rich dramatic custom, and guests to the nation can appreciate everything from conventional Kabuki and Noh exhibitions to contemporary plays and musicals. Tokyo's Ginza region is home to a few theaters, including the well-known Kabuki-za Theater, while Osaka's Public Bunraku Theater is eminent for its puppetry exhibitions.

AMUSEMENT PARKS

Japan is home to a portion of the world's most well-known amusement parks, including Tokyo Disneyland and Widespread Studios Japan. These parks are open until quite a bit later, permitting guests to encounter the attractions and shows into the evening.

NIGHT MARKETS

Night markets are a well-known fascination in Japan, particularly throughout the late spring months. These business sectors offer an extensive variety of food, drink, and shopping choices, and are an incredible method for encountering the nearby culture and nightlife.

All in all, Japan offers an extensive variety of evening diversion choices to suit all interests and spending plans. Whether you're hoping to sing your heart out at karaoke, partake in an unrecorded music execution, or experience customary theater, Japan has something for everybody.

CHAPTER NINE

DAY TRIPS FROM MAJOR CITIES IN JAPAN

Japan is a country with a rich history, various cultures, and dazzling normal magnificence. The nation is home to a few significant urban communities that offer an abundance of attractions and exercises for guests. In any case, probably the most astonishing encounters in Japan can be tracked down right outside these urban areas. Here are some times or other excursions from significant urban communities in Japan that you can consider:

ROAD TRIP FROM TOKYO: NIKKO
Nikko is a humble community situated around 2 hours from Tokyo and is well known for its UNESCO World Legacy Site, the Toshogu Hallowed place. The hallowed place is devoted to the organizer behind the Tokugawa Shogunate and is famous for its perplexing carvings and designs. Other than the sanctuary, Nikko has lovely normal scenes, underground aquifers, and climbing trails.

ROAD TRIP FROM KYOTO: NARA

Nara was the principal capital of Japan and is well known for its sanctuaries, hallowed places, and memorable destinations. It is just 45 minutes from Kyoto and is home to the Todaiji Sanctuary, which houses an enormous bronze Buddha sculpture, as well as numerous other noteworthy and social fortunes.

ROAD TRIP FROM OSAKA: HIMEJI

Himeji is home to perhaps Japan's most popular and delightful palace, the Himeji Palace. The palace is a UNESCO World Legacy Site and is one of a handful of enduring unique Japanese palaces. It is about an hour from Osaka and is a famous road trip destination.

ROAD TRIP FROM HIROSHIMA: MIYAJIMA

Miyajima is an island situated about an hour from Hiroshima and is popular for its Itsukushima Sanctum, which is based on the water and is a UNESCO World Legacy Site. The island is likewise home to a few climbing trails, dazzling views, and various neighborhood food sources.

ROAD TRIP FROM SAPPORO: OTARU

Otaru is a little port town situated around 40 minutes from Sapporo and is known for its wonderful trench, memorable structures, and fish. The town has a few historical centers and craftsmanship exhibitions, making it an ideal objective for workmanship darlings.

ROAD TRIP FROM NAGOYA: INUYAMA

Inuyama is a little city situated a short way from Nagoya and is known for its lovely palace, the Inuyama Palace. The palace is quite possibly the most seasoned enduring Japanese palace and is an assigned Irreplaceable asset. The city likewise has a customary Japanese road with old-style shops and cafés.

ROAD TRIP FROM FUKUOKA: YANAGAWA

Yanagawa is a city situated a little ways from Fukuoka and is popular for its waterways and customary Japanese boats, called donks boats. Guests can take a boat ride through the waterways while partaking in the view and finding out about the historical backdrop of the city.

ROAD TRIP FROM KOBE: HIMEJI

Himeji Palace, referenced above, is likewise effectively open from Kobe. Other than the palace, the city of Himeji has numerous other noteworthy destinations, for example, the Kokoen Nursery, a conventional Japanese nursery with various plants and lakes.

ROAD TRIP FROM SENDAI: MATSUSHIMA

Matsushima is a seaside town situated a little ways from Sendai and is known for its picturesque cove and the Matsushima Islands. Guests can take a boat visit around the islands and partake in the perspectives on the remarkable stone developments and sanctuaries.

ROAD TRIP FROM OKINAWA: ZAMAMI ISLAND

Zamami Island is a little island situated about an hour from Okinawa and is known for its delightful sea shores and coral reefs. Guests can go swimming or scuba plunging to see the energetic marine life or take a comfortable climb on the islands to tend paths.

Japan has various road trip choices for guests to investigate, and every city has its remarkable attractions and encounters. Whether you are keen on history, culture, or nature, or simply need to get away from the buzzing about the city, there is a road trip for everybody to appreciate.

DAY TRIP OPTIONS FROM TOKYO (E.G. NIKKO, KAMAKURA, YOKOHAMA)

Tokyo is a clamoring city that offers an exceptional blend of conventional and current culture. Notwithstanding, assuming you're hoping to get away from the rushing about of the city, there are a lot of road trip choices accessible that will permit you to investigate the encompassing regions. Here are probably the greatest road trip choices from Tokyo:

1. **Nikko**: Nikko is a modest community situated in the Tochigi Prefecture, around two hours north of Tokyo. It's known for its lovely sanctuaries and hallowed places, including the renowned Toshogu Sanctuary, which is a UNESCO World Legacy Site. Nikko

is likewise encircled by lovely nature, making it a famous object for climbing and open-air exercises.

2. **Kamakura**: Kamakura is a seaside town situated about an hour south of Tokyo. It's known for its numerous sanctuaries and holy places, including the popular Extraordinary Buddha of Kamakura, which is a bronze sculpture that stands more than 13 meters tall. Kamakura is additionally known for its lovely seashores and climbing trails.

3. **Yokohama**: Yokohama is a port city situated around 30 minutes south of Tokyo. It's known for its cosmopolitan energy and delightful waterfront region, which incorporates the renowned Minato Mirai 21 area. Yokohama is likewise home to the biggest Chinatown in Japan, as well as numerous galleries and social attractions.

4. **Mount Takao**: Mount Takao is a well-known climbing objective situated about an hour west of Tokyo. It's known for its delightful perspectives on the encompassing region, including Tokyo Sky tree and Mount Fuji.

There are a few climbing trails accessible, going from simple to troublesome, and the mountain is likewise home to a monkey park and a delightful sanctuary.

5. **Hakone**: Hakone is an uneven district situated around two hours southwest of Tokyo. It's known for its lovely regular landscape, including underground aquifers, lakes, and mountains. Hakone is additionally home to a few historical centers and social attractions, including the Hakone Outside Exhibition hall and the Hakone Place of worship.

These are only a couple of the numerous road trip choices accessible from Tokyo. Whether you're keen on investigating customary Japanese culture, lovely regular views, or present-day city life, there's something for everybody simply a brief excursion away from the city.

DAY TRIP OPTIONS FROM KYOTO (E.G. NARA, OSAKA, HIROSHIMA)

Kyoto, the previous magnificent capital of Japan, is an optimal base for investigating the Kansai district of Japan. While there's no deficiency of activities in Kyoto, it's likewise simple to make road trips to local objections. Here are some famous road trip choices from Kyoto:

1. **Nara**: Simply a short train ride away from Kyoto, Nara is renowned for its old sanctuaries, hallowed places, and cordial deer that wander uninhibitedly through the city. Visit Todaiji Sanctuary, the biggest wooden structure on the planet, and its goliath Buddha sculpture, as well as Kasuga Taisha, a UNESCO World Legacy Site.

2. **Osaka**: Known as the "Kitchen of Japan," Osaka is a food sweetheart's heaven. Test nearby fortes, for example, takoyaki (octopus balls), okonomiyaki (appetizing flapjacks), and kushikatsu (pan-fried sticks). Investigate attractions, for example, Osaka Palace, the Dotonbori amusement area, and the Umeda Sky Building.

3. **Hiroshima**: Albeit a piece further away from Kyoto, Hiroshima merits the excursion. Find

out about the city's unfortunate history at the Hiroshima Harmony Commemoration Park and Historical center, then, at that point, attempt the nearby claim to fame, Hiroshima-style okonomiyaki. Take a ship to Miyajima Island to see the renowned "drifting" torii entryway at Itsukushima Place of worship.

4. **Himeji**: Visit the shocking Himeji Palace, a UNESCO World Legacy Site and perhaps Japan's most notable milestone. Nicknamed the "White Heron Palace" for its white outside and elegant plan, Himeji Palace is one of the most mind-blowing preserved instances of archaic Japanese palace engineering.

5. **Kinosaki Onsen:** Loosen up in the underground aquifers of Kinosaki Onsen, a pleasant town in Hyogo Prefecture known for its seven public bathhouses. Walk around the roads in a yukata (a relaxed summer kimono) and test nearby fish.

These are only a couple of the numerous road trip choices from Kyoto. With phenomenal transportation connections, there is a lot to see and do in the Kansai district, so you won't ever be exhausted during your visit to Kyoto.

DAY TRIP OPTIONS FROM OTHER MAJOR CITIES IN JAPAN

Japan is a nation loaded up with entrancing objections and sights that are worth investigating. While remaining in any significant city, it's feasible to require a road trip to local locations to encounter the magnificence and appeal of Japan's open country. Here are a few choices for road trips from significant urban communities in Japan:

ROAD TRIP FROM TOKYO: NIKKO

Nikko is a UNESCO World Legacy Site and a famous road trip object from Tokyo. Situated in Tochigi Prefecture, Nikko is known for its beautiful places of worship and sanctuaries, encompassed by rich woodlands and mountains. The most popular of these is the Toshogu Place of worship, which is committed to Tokugawa Ieyasu, the organizer behind the Tokugawa Shogunate.

ROAD TRIP FROM KYOTO: NARA

Nara is an enchanting city that was once the capital of Japan. Found under an hour from Kyoto, Nara is known for its old sanctuaries, lovely nurseries, and agreeable deer that meander uninhibitedly in the city's parks. Perhaps the most well-known fascination in Nara is the Todai-ji Sanctuary, which houses a gigantic bronze sculpture of Buddha.

ROAD TRIP FROM OSAKA: HIMEJI PALACE

Himeji Palace is quite possibly one of Japan's most well-known palaces and is situated in Hyogo Prefecture, under an hour from Osaka. The palace is known for its wonderful white walls and great protective elements, which made it secure during fights in primitive Japan. Guests can move to the highest point of the palace for dazzling perspectives on the encompassing region.

ROAD TRIP FROM HIROSHIMA: MIYAJIMA

Miyajima is a little island found simply off the bank of Hiroshima, well known for its pleasant Torii entryway and wonderful view. The island is home to the Itsukushima Hallowed place, which is a

UNESCO World Legacy Site, and guests can appreciate climbing, cycling, and kayaking around the island.

ROAD TRIP FROM SAPPORO: OTARU

Otaru is an enchanting port town found under an hour from Sapporo. The town is known for its verifiable structures, waterways, and glassworks, making it an extraordinary objective for those keen on Japanese history and culture. Guests can likewise test the town's renowned fish and visit neighborhood markets and historical centers.

ROAD TRIP FROM FUKUOKA: DAZAIFU

Dazaifu is a modest community found right beyond Fukuoka, known for its verifiable importance and regular magnificence. The town is home to the Dazaifu Tenmangu Hallowed place, which is committed to the lord of learning, and guests can likewise appreciate climbing and investigating the close by mountains and woods.

These are only a couple of the numerous road trip choices accessible from significant urban communities in Japan. With its rich history, staggering scenes, and exceptional culture, Japan offers something for everybody, and road trips are an incredible method for encountering all that this interesting nation brings to the table.

CHAPTER TEN

FESTIVALS AND EVENTS IN JAPAN

Japan is a nation known for its lively and novel celebrations and occasions. The Japanese schedule is brimming with conventional festivals that mirror the country's rich history, social legacy, and strict convictions. Here are probably the most huge and well-known celebrations and occasions in Japan.

1. **New Year's Day (January first):** New Year's Day, or Shogatsu, is perhaps the most significant and generally celebrated occasion in Japan. Individuals visit holy places and sanctuaries to appeal to God for good well-being and fortune, and numerous families accumulate to eat conventional New Year's dishes, for example, ozone (soup with mochi rice cakes) and osechi (arranged dishes served in unique boxes).

2. **Setsubun (February third or fourth):** Setsubun marks the start of spring in Japan, and it's a chance to drive away detestable spirits and welcome the best of luck.

Individuals toss simmered soybeans while yelling "Oni wa soto! Fuku wa uchi!" (Out with devils, in with best of luck!) And eat ehomaki (sushi rolls) peacefully while confronting the fortunate heading of the year.

3. **Hinamatsuri (Walk third):** Hinamatsuri, or Young ladies' Day, is a celebration that commends the well-being and bliss of little kids. Families with little girls show a bunch of decorative dolls addressing the Head, Sovereign, and their court in conventional Heian period ensembles, and eat unique food sources, for example, chirashizushi (dissipated sushi) and hina-arare (glossed-over rice wafers).

4. **Hanami (Walk to April):** Hanami is when individuals accumulate under cherry bloom trees to see the value in their excellence and praise the appearance of spring. It's a well-known time for picnics, gatherings, and photography meetings, and a few popular spots for hanami incorporate Ueno Park, Meguro Waterway, and Mount Yoshino.

5. **Brilliant Week (Late April to Early May):** Brilliant Week is a progression of public occasions that happen in no less than seven days in late April and early May, including Showa Day (April 29th), Constitution Remembrance Day (May third), Plant life Day (May fourth), and Youngsters' Day (May fifth). Many individuals exploit extended vacations to travel or visit their families.

6. **Tanabata (July seventh):** Tanabata, or Star Celebration, is a heartfelt celebration that commends the gathering of two darlings, Orihime and Hikoboshi, who are isolated by the Smooth Way and can meet once a year on this day. Individuals compose their desires on tanzaku (vivid paper strips) and balance them on bamboo branches, and appreciate summer treats, for example, kakigori (shaved ice) and yukata (light cotton kimono).

7. **Obon (Mid-August):** Obon is a Buddhist celebration that respects the spirits of predecessors who return to the universe of the living for a concise period. Individuals clean their homes and visit their family

graves, and there are conventional moves called Bon Odori acting in nearby networks.

8. **Tokyo Game Show (September)**: The Tokyo Game Show is one of the biggest and most powerful computer game exhibitions on the planet. It includes the most recent games, control center, and advances from Japanese and global game organizations, and draws in gamers, industry experts, and aficionados from everywhere in the world.

9. **Jidai Matsuri (October 22nd):** Jidai Matsuri, or Celebration of Ages, is a verifiable celebration that features the social and authentic legacy of Kyoto, the previous capital of Japan. It includes an excellent motorcade of individuals in verifiable outfits addressing various times in Japanese history and incorporates exhibitions, displays, and functions.

10. **Halloween (October 31st):** Even though Halloween is not a customary Japanese celebration, it has acquired fame lately, particularly among youngsters. Many amusement parks, malls, and bars hold

Halloween occasions and gatherings, and individuals spruce up in ensembles and go house to house asking for candy.

11. **Shichi-Go-San (November fifteenth):** Shichi-Go-San, or Seven-Five-Three, is a conventional celebration that commends the development and prosperity of youngsters who are seven, five, or three years of age. Guardians dress their kids in conventional outfits and take them to sanctuaries or sanctuaries to appeal to God for their well-being and joy, and take dedicatory photographs.

12. **Christmas (December 25th):** Even though Christmas is not a strict occasion in Japan, it is broadly celebrated as a mainstream occasion. It's a period for present giving, heartfelt dates, and Christmas enlightenments, and numerous families appreciate Christmas cake and seared chicken for their extraordinary feast.

13. **Omisoka (December 31st):** Omisoka, or New Year's Eve, is a period for cleaning and planning for the New Year. Individuals eat

Toshi Koshi soba (buckwheat noodles) to represent life span and best of luck and watch the Kohaku Uta Gassen, a well-known music show on television that highlights exhibitions by popular Japanese vocalists and gatherings.

These are only a portion of the numerous celebrations and occasions that happen all through the year in Japan. They offer a brief look into the rich social customs and present-day patterns of this interesting country.

OVERVIEW OF POPULAR FESTIVALS AND EVENTS IN JAPAN (E.G. CHERRY BLOSSOM SEASON, GOLDEN WEEK, SUMMER FESTIVALS)

Japan is a country that is known for its rich culture and custom, which is reflected in the different celebrations and occasions that are commended over time. These celebrations and occasions offer guests a brief look into the country's novel legacy and customs. In this outline, we will feature probably the most famous celebrations and occasions in Japan.

1. **Cherry Bloom Season (late Walk to early May):** The cherry bloom, or sakura, is perhaps Japan's most notorious image, and its blossoming is praised across the country. During this time, individuals accumulate in parks and gardens to partake in the lovely pink and white blossoms, have picnics, and participate in customary exercises, for example, hanami (bloom seeing).

2. **Brilliant Week (late April to early May):** This is a seven-day extended vacation period in Japan that incorporates four public occasions, and it is one of the most active seasons for movement and the travel industry. Numerous Japanese individuals make a move to go inside the nation, and famous objections incorporate Tokyo, Kyoto, and Hokkaido.

3. **Summer Celebrations (July and August):** Summer celebrations, or matsuri, are held all through Japan during the sweltering and muggy long periods of July and August. These celebrations normally include road marches, conventional food and beverages, and light shows. Probably the most well-

known summer celebrations remember the Gion Matsuri for Kyoto, the Tenjin Matsuri in Osaka, and the Nebuta Matsuri in Aomori.

4. **Obon (mid-August):** Obon is a conventional Japanese Buddhist celebration that is held to respect the spirits of precursors. During this time, individuals return to the places where they grew up and see family graves to offer their appreciation. The celebration is additionally set apart by customary moves, called bon odori, which are performed to invite the spirits of precursors.

5. **Shichi-go-san (November 15):** Shichi-go-san, which signifies "seven-five-three," is a customary transitional experience for kids in Japan. Young men and young ladies who are seven, five, or three years of age spruce up in customary apparel and visit altars to get endowments for good well-being and satisfaction.

6. **New Year's Eve and New Year's Day (December 31 to January 1):** New Year's Eve and New Year's Day are commended with numerous conventional traditions and

customs in Japan. Individuals clean their homes and adorn them with customary trimmings, and they visit altars and sanctuaries to offer petitions for the approaching year. On New Year's Day, it is standard to eat soba noodles for a life span and to visit loved ones.

Generally speaking, Japan has a rich and varied social schedule loaded up with celebrations and occasions that offer guests a remarkable understanding of the nation's set of experiences, customs, and customs. Whether you are keen on the normal excellence of the cherry blooms, the energy of summer celebrations, or the profound meaning of Obon, there is something for everybody in Japan.

TIPS FOR ATTENDING FESTIVALS AND EVENTS IN JAPAN

Japan is known for its energetic and remarkable celebrations and occasions, which draw in a large number of guests consistently. Going to these celebrations can be an amazing encounter, yet it can likewise be overpowering if you don't have the foggiest idea of what's in store. Here are a few ways to go to celebrations and occasions in Japan:

1. **Research the occasion ahead of time:** Before going to any occasion or celebration, examine to find out about its set of experiences, customs, and customs. Knowing what's in store will assist you with valuing the experience and staying away from any social tactless act.

2. **Dress fittingly:** Numerous celebrations and occasions in Japan are held outside, so make a point to likewise dress. Wear agreeable shoes and garments that you wouldn't fret about getting filthy. Contingent upon the occasion, you may likewise be expected to wear a conventional dress, for example, a yukata or kimono.

3. **Show up before the expected time:** Japanese celebrations are known for being packed, so show up sooner than expected to keep away from the groups and get a decent spot. A few celebrations might try to begin before dawn, so be ready to get up right on

time if you have any desire to encounter the full occasion.

4. **Regarding the traditions:** Japanese celebrations frequently have exceptional traditions and customs, for example, purging ceremonies or the tossing of rice cakes. Regard these traditions and take an interest assuming you feel open to doing as such.

5. **Remain hydrated and filled:** Japanese celebrations can be a long and tiring day, so make a point to carry a lot of water and snacks to keep you energized over the day. It's likewise really smart to carry a little towel to wipe away perspiration.

6. **Be aware of others:** Japanese celebrations are a common encounter, so be aware of others around you. Try not to push or push, and be respectful to the people who might be more modest or less truly capable.

7. **Remember the camera:** Japanese celebrations are known for their beautiful and lively showcases, so remember to carry a camera to catch the recollections. Simply

be aware of the guidelines, as certain occasions might restrict photography.

8. **Plan transportation ahead of time:** Celebrations and occasions in Japan can draw in enormous groups, so plan your transportation ahead of time to abstain from stalling out in rush hour gridlock or passing up the occasion. Think about taking public transportation or strolling if conceivable.

9. **Know about well-being**: While celebrations and occasions in Japan are by and large protected, it's generally smart to know about your environmental factors and avoid potential risks to guarantee your security. Keep your resources close and be aware of pickpockets in packed regions.

10. **Become familiar with a few essential Japanese expressions**: While many individuals in Japan communicate in English, learning a few fundamental Japanese expressions can go quite far in making your experience more charming. Basic expressions like "hi," "thank you," and "excuse me" can assist you with speaking

with local people and showing your appreciation for their way of life.

11.**Regarding the climate**: Celebrations and occasions in Japan frequently include a great deal of waste, for example, food bundling and expendable utensils. Assist with limiting your effect on the climate by appropriately discarding your junk and utilizing reusable compartments and utensils if conceivable.

12.**Investigate the encompassing region:** Numerous celebrations and occasions in Japan happen in beautiful areas, so find an opportunity to investigate the encompassing region and value the excellence of Japan's regular scene. You might try and find unexpected, yet invaluable treasures that you could not have possibly in any case seen.

In rundown, going to celebrations and occasions in Japan can be a fantastic encounter. By doing some exploration ahead of time, dressing fittingly, showing up sooner than expected, regarding customs, remaining hydrated and filled, being aware of others, and bringing a camera, you'll make certain to have a critical and charming time.

CHAPTER ELEVEN

JAPAN WITH KIDS

Japan is a brilliant destination for families with kids, offering an intriguing blend of current innovation, old culture, delightful food, and a lot of open-air exercises. Here are some thoughts for a family-accommodating excursion to Japan:

1. **Visit Tokyo Disneyland and DisneySea:** Japan's Disneyland and DisneySea are two of the most famous amusement parks on the planet, and they are particularly adored by youngsters. Tokyo Disneyland offers exemplary Disney attractions, while DisneySea has a nautical topic with interesting rides and shows. The two parks are effectively available from Tokyo by open transportation.

2. **Investigate Kyoto's sanctuaries and nurseries:** Kyoto is home to numerous delightful sanctuaries and nurseries that are amazing to grown-ups, yet additionally interesting to kids. The Fushimi Inari Place of

worship is particularly well known, with its winding ways fixed with a huge number of radiant orange torii entryways. The close Arashiyama Bamboo Woods is likewise an unquestionable necessity.

3. **Find out about samurai and ninja history:** Children will cherish finding out about Japan's antiquated samurai and ninja champions. Tokyo's Samurai Gallery has presentations of shields and blades, as well as live shows. In Kyoto, the Ninjadera Sanctuary offers a special ninja experience with a directed visit and intelligent displays.

4. **Play with robots and innovation:** Japan is known for its state-of-the-art innovation, and there are many spots where children can see and connect with robots and other modern contraptions. The Miraikan Science Gallery in Tokyo has a scope of shows on mechanical technology, and space investigation, and that's just the beginning. The Robot Eatery in Tokyo is a wild and vivid show highlighting robots, artists, and lasers.

5. **Attempt Japanese food:** Japanese cooking is tasty and sound, and there are a lot of youngster-accommodating choices like sushi, ramen, and tempura. Numerous eateries have English menus and are acquainted with serving families with kids. In Tokyo, try the Tsukiji External Market for new fish and road food, and the Harajuku region for stylish desserts and bites.

6. **Go on a nature experience:** Japan is likewise home to numerous wonderful normal scenes, from the mountains to the ocean. The Fuji Five Lakes district offers climbing and trekking with valuable open doors with dazzling perspectives on Mount Fuji. The Okinawa islands have completely clear waters ideal for swimming and swimming with beautiful fish and ocean turtles.

Japan is a tomfoolery and instructive objective for families with children, and there are vast things to see and do. With its mix of conventional culture and current innovation, there's something for everybody to appreciate.

FAMILY-FRIENDLY ACTIVITIES AND ATTRACTIONS IN JAPAN

Japan is an extraordinary location for families searching for an intriguing and improving excursion experience. With its rich social legacy, regular excellence, and current attractions, Japan offers something for everybody. Here are a few family-accommodating exercises and attractions to consider:

1. **Tokyo Disneyland and DisneySea:** Tokyo Disneyland and DisneySea are two of the most famous attractions for families in Japan. These amusement parks offer different rides, shows, and attractions that make certain to charm youngsters and grown-ups the same.

2. **All-inclusive Studios Japan:** Widespread Studios Japan is another famous amusement park that offers a scope of rides and attractions in light of well-known films and Television programs.

3. **KidZania Tokyo:** KidZania Tokyo is an indoor amusement park where youngsters can

encounter various positions and callings in a reasonable and fun climate. Children can take a shot at being a specialist, fireman, cook, or even a pilot.

4. **Ghibli Gallery:** The Ghibli Exhibition hall is a must-visit fascination for fanatics of the Japanese movement. This gallery highlights shows and shows connected by Studio Ghibli, including the well-known films Vivacious Away and My Neighbor Totoro.

5. **Tokyo Skytree:** The Tokyo Skytree is the tallest pinnacle in Japan and offers all-encompassing perspectives on the city. Families can take a lift to the top for an outright exhilarating encounter and partake in the stunning perspectives.

6. **Mount Fuji:** Mount Fuji is perhaps Japan's most notable milestone and a UNESCO World Legacy Site. Families can take a directed visit or climb to the highest point for a stunning perspective on the encompassing scene.

7. **Osaka Aquarium Kaiyukan**: Osaka Aquarium Kaiyukan is one of the biggest aquariums on the planet and is home to the north of 30,000 marine creatures. Families can stroll through a passage encompassed by ocean animals and partake in different intuitive displays.

8. **Kyoto's Arashiyama Bamboo Forest:** The Arashiyama Bamboo Woods is a serene and picturesque objective in Kyoto. Families can stroll through the forest and partake in the tranquil environmental factors.

9. **Robot Café:** The Robot Eatery in Tokyo is an extraordinary and engaging experience that includes a show with monster robots, artists, and neon lights.

10. **Ninja Town in Iga:** The Ninja Town in Iga is a tomfoolery and instructive experience where families can find out about the historical backdrop of ninjas and take a stab at tossing shuriken (ninja stars) or partaking in a ninja impediment course.

In rundown, Japan offers an abundance of family-accommodating exercises and attractions. Whether you are keen on amusement parks, social encounters, or normal magnificence, Japan brings something to the table for all ages.

TIPS FOR TRAVELING TO JAPAN WITH KIDS (E.G. CHILD-FRIENDLY ACCOMMODATIONS, TRANSPORTATION OPTIONS, FOOD OPTIONS)

Japan is a magnificent destination to visit with youngsters. The nation is known for its inviting society, heavenly food, dazzling sights, and extraordinary encounters that make certain to enamor youthful voyagers. Here are some ways to go to Japan with children to guarantee a tomfoolery and peaceful excursion.

1. **Pick Youngster cordial Facilities:** While booking facilities, search for inns or rental homes that are kid agreeable. Numerous inns offer conveniences like dens, child baths, and high seats, as well as youngsters' play regions and games. Consider booking a room with a kitchenette so you can get ready bites or feasts for your kids.

2. **Decide on Open Transportation:** Japan's public transportation framework is effective and all around kept up with. Think about utilizing trains, metros, or transports to get around, as they are not difficult to explore and offer a lot of room for buggies and gear. Most trains have assigned regions for buggies, and many stations have lifts or elevators to make it more straightforward to move around with kids.

3. **Plan Your Schedule Admirably**: Going with kids requires more preparation than traveling alone. Consider restricting the number of exercises you plan every day and booking a lot of margin time. Additionally, make certain to incorporate exercises that are important to your kids, for example, visiting event congregations or creature bistros.

4. **Attempt Youngster Cordial Food varieties:** Japan has an amazing culinary scene, yet it could be scary for particular eaters or kids who are not used to Japanese cooking. Notwithstanding, numerous Japanese food

sources are amicable, for example, ramen, tempura, sushi rolls, and yakitori (barbecued chicken sticks). You can likewise find Western-style cheap food chains in the greater urban areas.

5. **Bring Tidbits and Beverages:** It's dependably really smart to have bites and beverages close by, particularly assuming you're going with small kids who might get eager or parched in a hurry. Japanese corner shops, or "Konbini," have a wide choice of tidbits, beverages, and prepared-to-eat feasts that are ideal for families in a hurry.

6. **Visit Youngster Agreeable Attractions**: Japan has numerous attractions that are ideally suited for youngsters, for example, Tokyo Disneyland and DisneySea, General Studios Japan, and the Ghibli Exhibition hall. There are likewise a lot of parks, zoos, and aquariums that offer intuitive displays and exercises for youngsters.

7. **Exploit Youngster Limits:** Numerous attractions in Japan offer limited affirmation costs for kids. Make certain to take a look at

every fascination's site or get some information about kid limits. Some train organizations additionally offer limited charges for kids.

Going to Japan with children can be a magnificent encounter that makes enduring recollections. By following these tips, you can guarantee a calm excursion that is fun and charming for the entire family.

CHAPTER TWELVE

ECO-TOURISM IN JAPAN

With the rising attention to manageable the travel industry, eco-the travel industry has acquired ubiquity lately. Eco-the travel industry is a type of travel industry that elevates mindful travel to normal regions while limiting adverse consequences on the climate and supporting protection endeavors.

Japan brings a great deal to the table for eco-travelers, with its different regular excellence, rich culture, and eco-accommodating practices. The nation has various public parks and UNESCO World Legacy Destinations that draw in a huge number of sightseers consistently. A portion of the famous eco-the travel industry objections in Japan include:

1. **Yakushima Island**: Yakushima is a little island situated off the southern shore of Japan. The island is renowned for its antiquated cedar woodlands, which are north of 1,000 years of age. The backwoods are a UNESCO World Legacy Site and home

to uncommon types of widely varied vegetation, like the Yakushima macaque and the Yakushima deer.

2. **Shiretoko Landmass:** Shiretoko is a promontory situated in the northeastern piece of Hokkaido, Japan's northernmost island. The landmass is a UNESCO World Legacy Site known for its immaculate wilderness, including the Shiretoko Five Lakes and the Kamuiwakka Falls. Guests can likewise recognize different natural life, including earthy-colored bears, deer, and foxes.

3. **Mount Fuji:** Mount Fuji is Japan's tallest mountain and a UNESCO World Legacy Site. The mountain is encircled by beautiful scenes and draws in a great many guests consistently. Eco-sightseers can appreciate climbing, setting up camp, and birdwatching nearby.

4. **Ishigaki Island:** Ishigaki is in Okinawa Prefecture, Japan's southernmost prefecture. The island is known for its coral reefs, which are home to various types of

marine life, for example, ocean turtles, manta beams, and whale sharks. Guests can go swimming or plunging to investigate the submerged world.

Notwithstanding these normal attractions, Japan has additionally executed a few eco-accommodating practices to help support the travel industry. For instance, the nation has a proficient public transportation framework, including trains and transport, which lessens the requirement for rental vehicles and limits fossil fuel byproducts. Numerous facilities in Japan likewise use eco-accommodating practices, for example, energy-proficient lighting and water-saving gadgets.

All in all, the eco-the travel industry is a developing pattern in Japan, with numerous normal attractions and eco-accommodating practices. Guests can partake in the country's rich culture and normal excellence while supporting preservation endeavors and limiting adverse consequences on the climate.

ECO-FRIENDLY TOURISM OPTIONS IN JAPAN (E.G. HIKING, CAMPING, WILDLIFE WATCHING)

Japan is a country with a rich social legacy and staggering normal magnificence. With a rising spotlight on maintainability, eco-accommodating the travel industry choices have become more well-known as of late. Here are some eco-accommodating travel industry choices in Japan that voyagers can consider:

1. **Climbing**: Japan has a broad organization of climbing trails, going from simple strolls to testing multi-day journeys. Climbing is an incredible method for encountering the regular magnificence of Japan, from the lavish woodlands of Hokkaido to the volcanic pinnacles of Kyushu. A considerable lot of these paths are very much kept up with and offer stupendous perspectives on the encompassing scene. Moreover, climbing is a low-influence movement that permits voyagers to encounter the magnificence of nature while limiting its ecological effect.

2. **Setting up camp:** Setting up camp is an extraordinary method for interfacing with

nature and partaking in the serenity of Japan's wild regions. Japan has numerous campgrounds that are available by open transportation, making it simple for voyagers to get off the generally accepted way to go and encounter the magnificence of the country's normal regions. Also, numerous campgrounds offer eco-accommodating conveniences, for example, treating the soil latrines and reusing offices.

3. **Untamed life Watching:** Japan is home to a different scope of untamed life, including bears, monkeys, and deer. Untamed life-watching visits can be an extraordinary method for encountering these creatures in their normal natural surroundings while finding out about their behavior and preservation endeavors. It's vital to pick a visit administrator that works in an eco-accommodating way and focuses on creature government assistance.

4. **Onsen (Natural aquifers):** Japan is well known for its underground aquifers, which are accepted to have medical advantages and are a famous objective for the two local

people and vacationers. Nonetheless, it's vital to pick onsen that is earth capable, as a few natural aquifers utilize over-the-top measures of water and synthetic substances. Search for onsen that utilizes regular, mineral-rich water and focuses on supportability in their activities.

5. **Cycling**: Cycling is an incredible method for investigating Japan's urban communities and provincial regions while limiting your natural effect. Japan has a broad organization of cycling trails and bicycle rental offices, making it simple to investigate the country on two wheels. Moreover, cycling is a low-influence movement that can be delighted in by voyagers of any age and wellness level.

All in all, Japan offers an abundance of eco-accommodating travel industry choices for voyagers who need to encounter the country's regular magnificence while limiting its natural effect. From climbing and setting up camp to untamed life watching and onsen, there are numerous ways of getting a charge out of Japan economically and capably.

SUSTAINABLE TOURISM INITIATIVES IN JAPAN

Japan has taken critical steps towards advancing the travel industry lately. The nation has been proactive in creating and carrying out different drives pointed toward monitoring regular assets, lessening fossil fuel byproducts, and protecting the country's social legacy. Here are a few instances of maintainable the travel industry drives in Japan:

1. **Eco-the-travel industry:** Japan has an assortment of eco-the-travel industry choices, including public parks, nature stores, and untamed life safe-havens. Guests can partake in exercises, for example, climbing, bird-watching, and whale watching while at the same time finding out about the neighborhood's biological systems and protection endeavors.

2. **Social travel industry:** Japan's rich social legacy is a huge draw for guests. Be that as it may, the nation is likewise dedicated to saving and reasonably advancing its social locales. For instance, guests can take part in conventional social exercises, for example, tea functions and calligraphy classes, which

support neighborhood craftsmen and advance social trade.

3. **Green inns:** Japan has been at the forefront of advancing harm to the ecosystem, with numerous lodgings embracing manageable practices like energy-proficient lighting, reusing programs, and privately obtained food.

4. **Public transportation:** Japan's public transportation framework is eminent for its productivity and dependability, making it an incredible choice for vacationers. By empowering guests to utilize public transportation, Japan can diminish fossil fuel byproducts and advance economical travel.

5. **Squander decrease**: Japan is known for its severe waste administration arrangements, which have assisted the country with keeping up with spotless and solid conditions. Numerous lodgings and traveler locales have embraced squander decrease drives, for example, treating the soil, reusing, and lessening single-use plastics.

6. **Local area based on the travel industry:**
   Japan has areas of strength for local areas based on the travel industry, where guests can encounter nearby culture and customs while supporting neighborhood networks. This approach advances the travel industry by giving financial advantages to nearby networks while limiting the effect on the climate.

All in all, Japan has carried out a different economy. The travel industry drives to advance capable travel while saving the nation's regular and social legacy. These drives have assisted with making the travel industry more, helping the two guests and the climate.

CHAPTER THIRTEEN

SPECIAL INTEREST IN TRAVEL IN JAPAN

Japan is a captivating country that has caught the creative mind of explorers all over the planet. From the clamoring urban communities of Tokyo and Osaka to the quiet sanctuaries of Kyoto and the cold slants of Hokkaido, there is something for everybody in Japan. Notwithstanding, for those with a particular interest, there are plenty of extraordinarily interesting travel choices accessible that can give a significantly more vivid experience.

Here are a few instances of exceptional interest travel choices in Japan:

1. **Food and Drink:** Japan is known for its remarkable cooking and the craft of feasting. A food and drink visit can take you on an excursion to investigate the country's numerous culinary pleasures, like sushi, ramen, and purpose, and that's just the beginning. You can visit food markets, go to cooking classes, and even stay at customary ryokans where dinners are incorporated.

2. **Anime and Manga:** For enthusiasts of anime and manga, Japan is a mecca. Many accessible visits can take you to well-known areas highlighted in famous anime series, like the Ghibli Exhibition hall, which has grandstands crafted by Studio Ghibli. You can likewise go to anime shows and meet renowned manga specialists.

3. **Customary Expressions and Specialties:** Japan has a rich history of conventional expressions and specialties, from earthenware to calligraphy to kimono production. You can visit studios and find out about the methods used to make these wonderful show-stoppers. A few visits even permit you to take a stab at making your conventional specialties.

4. **History and Culture:** Japan has a captivating history and culture that is saturated with custom. You can visit old sanctuaries and holy places, go to conventional celebrations, and find out about Japan's samurai history. You can likewise visit exhibition halls and craftsmanship displays to become familiar

with the nation's way of life and workmanship.

5. **Nature and Outside:** Japan has a different scene that reaches from cold mountains to tropical sea shores. You can go climbing, skiing, or snowboarding in the mountains, visit public parks to see the cherry blooms in spring or the harvest time leaves in fall, or even go scuba diving in Okinawa.

All in all, Japan offers an abundance of extraordinarily interesting travel choices for people who are searching for a more vivid and customized insight. Whether you are keen on food and drink, anime and manga, customary expressions and artworks, history and culture, or nature and outside, there is something for everybody in Japan.

OPTIONS FOR NICHE TRAVEL IN JAPAN (E.G. ANIME AND MANGA TOURS, FOOD AND DRINK TOURS, ART AND CULTURE TOURS)

Japan is a country with a rich culture, history, and a different scope of specialty interests. From anime and manga to food and craftsmanship, there are numerous choices for voyagers who need to investigate Japan's interesting contributions. Here are a few choices for specialty travel in Japan:

1. **Anime and Manga Visits:** Japan is known for the origination of anime and manga, and many fans run to the country to drench themselves in the way of life. Many visit administrators work in anime and manga visits, taking guests to well-known anime and manga spots, for example, Akihabara, Tokyo Anime Center, and Ghibli Exhibition hall. These visits frequently incorporate visits to anime and manga shops, cosplay occasions, and even voice acting classes.

2. **Food and Drink Visits:** Japan is a foodie's heaven, with a rich culinary culture that incorporates sushi, ramen, and tempura, and the sky's the limit from there. There are numerous food and drink visits accessible that take guests to neighborhood markets, road food slows down, and Michelin-featured eateries. Guests can likewise attempt purpose tasting visits, tea functions, and even figure out how to make their sushi.

3. **Workmanship and Culture Visits:** Japan has a rich history of craftsmanship and culture, from customary kabuki theater to contemporary workmanship exhibitions. Many visit administrators represent considerable authority in workmanship and culture visits, taking guests to well-known social milestones, for example, the sanctuaries of Kyoto, the Hiroshima Harmony Commemoration Park, and the Public Exhibition hall of Present-day Craftsmanship in Tokyo. Guests can likewise take part in conventional Japanese exercises like calligraphy, stoneware, and kimono dressing.

4. **Sports and Open-air Exercises:** Japan has various games and outside exercises that are novel to the country. Guests can partake in exercises, for example, sumo wrestling, judo, and kendo, or appreciate outside exercises like skiing, climbing, and surfing. There are likewise numerous natural aquifers (onsen) throughout the country, which are well-known objectives for unwinding and revival.

5. **Mainstream society Visits:** Japan is a center of mainstream society, from design to music to video games. Guests can take mainstream society visits that incorporate visits to popular design locales like Harajuku, music occasions, and computer game arcades. There are additionally numerous occasions during the time that celebrate mainstream society, for example, the Tokyo Game Show and the Comic Market.

Japan offers an extensive variety of specialty venture choices that take care of various interests and inclinations. Whether you're an anime fan, a foodie, a workmanship sweetheart, or a games devotee, there is something for everybody in Japan.

TIPS FOR PLANNING A SPECIAL INTEREST TRIP TO JAPAN

Arranging a unique interest excursion to Japan can be a thrilling and compensating experience, whether you are keen on food, history, culture, or some other part of this intriguing country. Be that as it may, with such a great amount to see and does, it can likewise be overpowering to choose where to go and what to see.

Here are a few hints to assist you with arranging an extraordinary interest outing to Japan:

1. **Pick your subject:** The most important phase in arranging an extraordinary interest outing to Japan is to pick your topic. What part of Japan would you say you are generally intrigued by? Is it true that you are keen on Japanese food, culture, history, or something different? Whenever you have settled on your subject, you can begin to explore the spots in Japan that are generally firmly connected with your advantage.

2. **Research your objections:** Whenever you have settled on your topic, research the objections in Japan that are generally firmly connected with your advantage. For instance, assuming you are keen on Japanese food, you might need to visit Tokyo, Osaka, and Kyoto, which are undeniably known for their extraordinary cooking.

3. **Plan your agenda**: Whenever you have settled on your objections, plan your schedule. Conclude how long you need to spend on every objective, and ensure you have sufficient opportunity to see all that you need to see. On the off chance that you are going during the top season, make certain to book your facilities and transportation well ahead of time.

4. **Consider recruiting an aide**: Assuming that you are keen on a particular part of Japanese culture or history, consider employing an aide who works in that space. An aide can furnish you with inside and out information and experiences that you may not get all alone.

5. **Pack fittingly**: Japan has a four-season environment, so make certain to pack suitably for the climate. You ought to likewise bring open-to-strolling shoes, as you will probably be doing a great deal of strolling and investigating.

6. **Regarding nearby traditions:** At long last, regarding neighborhood customs and

traditions is significant. This incorporates all that from removing your shoes while entering a home or sanctuary to not talking noisily on open transportation. By regarding nearby traditions, you will show your appreciation for Japanese culture and make your outing more charming for everybody.

7. **Buy a Japan Rail Pass:** If you intend to go around Japan via train, consider buying a Japan Rail Pass before you show up. This pass permits you to go on most trains in Japan for a proper period, which can save you a huge load of cash contrasted with purchasing individual tickets.

8. **Visit galleries and social destinations**: Japan is home to numerous historical centers and social locales so make certain to remember some for your schedule. Whether you are keen on conventional expressions and specialties, current craftsmanship, or history, there is something for everybody.

9. **Go to a celebration**: Japan is known for its celebrations, which are held consistently. From the renowned cherry bloom

celebrations in the spring to the beautiful fall leaves celebrations, there is continuously something to celebrate in Japan. Going to a celebration is an incredible method for encountering Japanese culture and meeting local people.

10. **Participate in a social encounter**: Many visit administrators offer social encounters, for example, tea functions, calligraphy classes, and sushi production classes. These encounters can give a more profound comprehension of Japanese culture and customs.

11. **Research the best opportunity to visit:** Japan has four particular seasons, and the best chance to visit relies upon your inclinations. Assuming you are keen on cherry blooms, visit in the spring. To see pre-winter leaves, visit in the fall. If you have any desire to stay away from swarms, think about visiting during the slow time of year.

12. **Consider a homestay or guesthouse:** Remaining with a neighborhood family or in a guesthouse can be an extraordinary

method for encountering Japanese culture and cordiality. You can get more familiar with day-to-day existence in Japan and get inside tips on the most ideal getaway spots.

All in all, arranging an extraordinary interest excursion to Japan requires some exploration and planning, however, it tends to be a staggeringly compensating experience. By picking your subject, exploring your objections, arranging your schedule, finding out about Japanese traditions and culture, attempting nearby food, pressing suitably, considering employing an aide, and regarding neighborhood customs, you can have a vital and pleasant excursion to Japan.

CHAPTER FOURTEEN

RESOURCES FOR TRAVEL TO JAPAN

Heading out to Japan can be an unbelievable encounter; however, it can likewise be overpowering, and particularly assuming you're going there interestingly. Luckily, there are numerous assets accessible to assist you with arranging your excursion and taking advantage of your time in Japan.

Here are a few assets to consider:

1. **Japan Public The travel industry Association (JNTO)** - The JNTO is the authority of the travel industry association for Japan and gives an abundance of data about the movement to Japan, including where to go, what to see, and how to get around. Their site offers travel guides, maps, and proposed agendas, and that's only the tip of the iceberg.

2. **Japan Guide** - Japan Guide is a complete site that gives data on all that you want to be

familiar with going to Japan, from transportation and convenience to touring and social encounters. They additionally offer discussions where you can get clarification on some pressing issues and get exhortation from different explorers.

3. **Hyperdia** - Hyperdia is a site and application that gives data on train timetables, courses, and tolls all through Japan. It's a fundamental device for getting around Japan, particularly assuming you're wanting to go via train.

4. **Japan Rail Pass** - The Japan Rail Pass is a practical method for going via train in Japan. It's simply accessible to unfamiliar sightseers and permits limitless travel on Japan Rail routes (JR) trains for a set period, generally 7, 14, or 21 days.

5. **Google Interpret** - While numerous Japanese individuals communicate in English, there are as yet numerous circumstances where a language boundary can challenge. Google Interpret is an amazing device for deciphering signs,

menus, and other composite materials into English (or some other language you like).

6. **Airbnb** - On the off chance that you're searching for an exceptional convenience experience in Japan, think about utilizing Airbnb. You can track down conventional Japanese homes, present-day lofts, and in the middle between. Remaining in an Airbnb can likewise allow you an opportunity to communicate with local people and get inside tips on what to see and do.

7. **Japan Travel Applications** - There are numerous helpful travel applications accessible for Japan, including applications for language interpretation, route, and touring. Some well-known applications incorporate NAVITIME for Japan Travel, Japan Associated free Wi-Fi, and the Tokyo Tram Route application.

Generally speaking, arranging an outing to Japan can be a tomfoolery and energizing interaction. By using the assets above, you can make a schedule that boosts your time in Japan and guarantees that you have a significant excursion.

RECOMMENDED GUIDEBOOKS AND TRAVEL WEBSITES

While arranging an outing, manuals, and travel sites can be very valuable assets for voyagers. They can give data on everything from facilities and cafés to nearby traditions and attractions. Here are a few prescribed manuals and travel sites to consider:

1. **Forlorn Planet** - Desolate Planet is a notable travel manual series that covers objections everywhere. Their manuals give natty gritty data on attractions, facilities, and eateries, from there, the sky's the limit. They likewise have a complete site that incorporates travel tips, objective aides, and a local area gathering.

2. **Rick Steves** - Rick Steves is a movement essayist and television character who centers on European travel. His manuals are known for their pragmatic exhortation and spending plan cordial proposals. His site likewise offers an abundance of data,

including travel tips, digital broadcasts, and visit data.

3. **Fodor's** - Fodor's has been distributing travel manuals beginning around 1936 and covers objections everywhere. Their manuals give definite data on attractions, facilities, and eateries, and that's just the beginning. Their site likewise offers travel tips, objective aides, and a local area gathering.

4. **TripAdvisor** - TripAdvisor is a movement site that gives surveys and suggestions from voyagers. The site incorporates audits of lodgings, cafés, and attractions, and that's only the tip of the iceberg. They likewise offer travel guides and booking administrations.

5. **Airbnb** - Airbnb is a site that permits explorers to book facilities in confidential homes and condos. They offer a scope of facilities, from spending plans well disposed to extravagance. The site additionally offers encounters and exercises driven by nearby have.

6. **Google Guides** - Google Guides is a planning administration that can be very helpful for voyagers. It offers bearings, travel data, and continuous traffic refreshes. It can likewise be utilized to track down eateries, attractions, and facilities.

7. **Booking.com** - Booking.com is a site that permits voyagers to book facilities all over the planet. They offer a scope of facilities, from spending plans well disposed to extravagance. The site additionally offers booking administrations for flights, rental vehicles, and exercises.

8. **Expedia** - Expedia is a site that permits voyagers to book flights, inns, rental vehicles, and exercises. They offer a scope of facilities, from financial plans well disposed to extravagance. The site likewise offers travel guides and a prizes program.

Generally, these manuals and travel sites can be very useful while arranging an outing. They can give important data, surveys, and suggestions, making it simpler to make informed conclusions about facilities, eateries, and attractions.

APPS AND TOOLS FOR TRAVELING IN JAPAN

For explorers, exploring through urban communities and tracking down the most ideal getaway destinations can be a piece of overpowering. Luckily, there are numerous applications and apparatuses accessible that can assist you with arranging your excursion and taking full advantage of your time in Japan. Here are probably the best applications and devices for going to Japan:

1. **Google Guides:** Google Guides is a valuable instrument for finding your strategy for getting around Japan, whether you're strolling, cycling, or driving. The application gives natty gritty guides, bearings, and data about open transportation choices. It likewise incorporates surveys and evaluations of eateries, lodgings, and different attractions, making it an incredible asset for arranging your excursion.

2. **Japan Travel by NAVITIME:** Japan Travel by NAVITIME is a complete travel guide that

covers all parts of the movement in Japan, including transportation, facilities, cafés, and touring. The application gives itemized data on famous traveler objections, as well as outside of what might be expected attractions that merit investigating. It likewise incorporates maps, photographs, and surveys, making it an extraordinary device for arranging your schedule.

3. **Japan Official Travel Application**: The Japan Official Travel Application is an across-the-board application that gives an abundance of data on Japan's vacationer locations, transportation, and facilities, and the sky's the limit from there. The application incorporates natty gritty advisers for Japan's significant urban communities, as well as data on less popular objections. It likewise incorporates an interpretation highlight that permits you to speak with local people in Japanese.

4. **Yomiwa**: Yomiwa is a valuable application for explorers who don't communicate in Japanese. The application utilizes your telephone's camera to examine Japanese

messages and give moment interpretations. It likewise incorporates a word reference and cheat sheet that can assist you with learning fundamental Japanese expressions.

5. **Tokyo Tram Route:** Tokyo Metro Route is a helpful application for exploring Tokyo's perplexing tram framework. The application gives natty gritty guides, schedules, and course organizers, making it simple to track down your strategy for getting around the city. It likewise remembers data for vacation spots and eateries close to metro stations.

6. **JapanTaxi**: JapanTaxi is a well-known application for booking taxis in Japan. The application permits you to book a taxi ahead of time or on request and gives a gauge of the charge. It likewise incorporates an element that permits you to speak with the driver in Japanese.

All in all, these applications and apparatuses can assist you with exploring Japan and taking full advantage of your excursion. Whether you're searching for train plans, bearings, interpretation administrations, or taxi booking, there's an application or device that can help you. With these instruments readily available, you'll have the option to investigate Japan effortlessly.

OTHER RESOURCES FOR PLANNING A TRIP TO JAPAN.

Arranging an excursion to Japan can be invigorating, however, it can likewise be overpowering given the countries numerous attractions, social subtleties, and strategic contemplations. Here are a few different assets you can use to design your outing to Japan:

1. **Japan Public The travel industry Association (JNTO)**: JNTO is the authority of the travel industry association of Japan and gives an abundance of data on the nation's attractions, occasions, facilities, and transportation. Its site (https://www.japan.travel/en/) offers a far-reaching guide for first-time guests and gives down-to-earth tips on all that from visa prerequisites to Japanese manners.

2. **Desolate Planet Japan:** Forlorn Planet is one of the most confided-in movement manual distributors, and their Japan manual is an extraordinary asset for arranging your outing. It remembers point-by-point data for famous objections, down-to-earth tips on transportation, convenience proposals, and social bits of knowledge.

3. **Japan Guide:** Japan Guide (https://www.japan-guide.com/) is an autonomous travel guide that offers far-reaching data on Japan's attractions, facilities, transportation, and culture. It likewise has a discussion where explorers can trade data and clarify some things.

4. **TripAdvisor**: TripAdvisor is a famous web-based survey stage that gives voyagers proposals for inns, cafés, and attractions in light of client audits. It tends to be a valuable device for tracking down the best places to remain and eat in Japan.

5. **HyperDia**: HyperDia (http://www.hyperdia.com/) is a site that gives continuous data on Japan's train

timetables, courses, and passages. This is a fundamental device for exploring Japan's broad rail organization, which is one of the most incredible ways of going around the country.

6. **Google Guides:** Google Guides is an incredible instrument for exploring Japan's urban communities and tracking down bearings. It likewise gives continuous data on open transportation timetables and courses.

7. **Japan Rail Pass:** If you anticipate going around Japan via train, the Japan Rail Pass is an unquestionable requirement. It permits limitless travel on Japan Rail lines (JR) trains for a set timeframe and can save you a truckload of cash contrasted with purchasing individual tickets.

8. **Japan Remote:** Japan Remote (https://japanwireless.com/) is an organization that gives pocket wifi and SIM card rental administrations for voyagers. Having web access while going to Japan can

be extremely useful for exploring and remaining associated.

All in all, arranging an excursion to Japan can be made simpler by utilizing these assets, yet there are a lot more out there. It's vital to properly investigate things and plan to guarantee you have the most ideal involvement with this intriguing and delightful country.

CHAPTER FIFTEEN

CONCLUSION

RECAP OF WHY JAPAN IS A GREAT TRAVEL DESTINATION

Japan is an extraordinary travel destination for several reasons. From its rich culture and history to its dazzling regular view and clamoring present-day urban communities, there is something for everybody to appreciate.

Here is a portion of the fundamental justifications for why Japan is an incredible travel objective:

1. **Rich Culture and History:** Japan has a long and intriguing history, with numerous old sanctuaries, hallowed places, and palaces to investigate. The nation is additionally known for its interesting practices, like tea services, geisha exhibitions, and sumo wrestling.

2. **Heavenly Food:** Japanese cooking is known all over the planet for its new fixings, exceptional flavors, and wonderful show. From sushi and sashimi to ramen and tempura, there are a lot of delightful dishes to try.

3. **Dazzling View:** Japan is home to probably the loveliest regular landscape on the planet, including Mount Fuji, cherry blossom trees, and vivid harvest-time foliage. There are likewise numerous natural aquifers and conventional Japanese nurseries to visit.

4. **Innovation and Advancement:** Japan is at the front line of innovation and development, with state-of-the-art improvements in fields like mechanical technology and transportation. Guests can

investigate modern urban communities like Tokyo and Osaka, which are loaded up with innovative contraptions and attractions.

5. **Warm Friendliness:** Japanese individuals are known for their agreeable and inviting nature, and guests to the nation can hope to be treated with thoughtfulness and regard.

6. **Interesting Mainstream society:** Japan is known all over the planet for its dynamic mainstream society, including anime, manga, and computer games. Guests can investigate locales like Akihabara and Harajuku, which are loaded up with shops and attractions devoted to these interests.

7. **Proficient Transportation:** Japan has one of the most effective and dependable transportation frameworks on the planet, including short trains (shinkansen) that can arrive at paces of up to 320 km/h. This makes it simple to go around the nation and see different objections during your outing.

8. **Security**: Japan is viewed as perhaps the most secure country on the planet, with low

degrees of wrongdoing and a solid feeling of social request. This makes it an incredible objective for solo explorers or families with small kids.

9. **Seasons and Celebrations:** Japan is known for its unmistakable seasons, each with its novel excellence and exercises. Guests can encounter cherry blossom season in the spring, firecrackers celebrations in the mid-year, pre-winter foliage in the fall, and snow celebrations in the colder time of year.

10. **Shopping**: Japan is a customer's heaven, with a large number of items accessible from customary specialties to state-of-the-art innovation. Famous shopping objects remember Ginza in Tokyo, Dotonbori in Osaka, and Nishiki Market in Kyoto.

In rundown, Japan is a movement objective that offers a remarkable mix of culture, history, nature, innovation, and cordiality. Guests can encounter everything from old sanctuaries and conventional food to advanced urban areas and mainstream society. With such a great amount to see and do, no big surprise Japan is a top travel destination for individuals all over the planet.

FINAL TIPS AND RECOMMENDATIONS FOR TRAVELING IN JAPAN.

Japan is a staggering objective, with an extraordinary mix of custom and innovation, and a culture that is entrancing to investigate. If you're arranging an outing to Japan, here are a few last tips and suggestions to assist you with capitalizing on your excursion:

1. **Become familiar with a couple of fundamental Japanese expressions:** Regardless of whether you communicate in Japanese easily, learning a couple of essential expressions like "hi", "thank you", and "excuse me" can go a long way toward helping you communicate with locals and understand their way of life.

2. **Follow neighborhood customs and behavior:** Japan has a rich culture and numerous exceptional traditions and customs, so it's critical to extend regard and

follow nearby manners. This includes removing your shoes while entering somebody's home or certain public spaces, bowing while saying hello to somebody, and staying away from clear or problematic conduct openly.

3. **Attempt neighborhood cooking:** Japan is known for its delectable food, from sushi and ramen to tempura and yakitori. Don't hesitate for even a moment to have a go at something new and embrace the nearby cooking - you may be shocked by the amount you appreciate it!

4. **Exploit public transportation:** Japan has a phenomenal public transportation framework, including trains, trams, and transport, that can take you to any place you need to go. It's frequently quicker and more advantageous than driving, so think about utilizing public transportation to get around.

5. **Plan your schedule cautiously:** Japan brings a ton to the table, from clamoring urban communities to peaceful open countries, so it's critical to design your agenda cautiously

to capitalize on your time. Consider which attractions and encounters are generally critical to you, and be reasonable about the amount you can squeeze into your timetable.

6. **Regarding neighborhood customs, while visiting hallowed places and sanctuaries**: Japan has numerous lovely sanctums and sanctuaries that are significant social and strict destinations. While visiting these spots, it's vital to extend consideration by taking off your shoes, covering your shoulders and legs, and shunning clear or problematic ways of behaving.

7. **Be ready for the climate:** Japan has a different environment, with blistering summers and cold winters, so it's critical to likewise pack. Check the weather conditions estimate before you proceed to bring suitable attire and embellishments, for example, an umbrella or sun cap.

8. **Make it a point to request help:** Japanese individuals are by and large cordial and supportive, so feel free to ask for headings

or help on the off chance that you want it. Many individuals talk in any event some English, and there are additional vacationer data focuses and help work areas at significant train stations and air terminals.

9. **Partake in the landscape:** Japan is a delightful country with a staggering normal view, from snow-covered mountains to cherry bloom-lined roads. Carve out the opportunity to see the value in the magnificence around you and partake in the slower speed of life in a portion of Japan's more rustic regions.

10. **Have some good times:** At last, remember to have a good time! Japan is an incredible objective with such a great amount to see and do, so carve out an opportunity to have a ball and make enduring recollections.

11. **Convey cash:** While Visas are acknowledged all things considered huge lodgings and stores in Japan, numerous more modest shops and cafés just acknowledge cash. Make certain to convey sufficient yen with

you to cover costs all through your excursion.

12.**Remain associated:** On the off chance that you want to remain associated while going to Japan, consider leasing a pocket Wi-Fi gadget or buying a SIM card for your telephone. This will permit you to get to the web and settle on decisions or send messages depending on the situation.

13.**Exploit far-reaching developments**: Japan has a rich social legacy, and there are numerous celebrations, occasions, and exhibitions during the time that offer a one-of-a-kind look into Japanese culture. Check nearby postings and traveler data to see what's going on during your outing.

14.**Regarding individual space**: Japan is a thickly populated nation, and individual space is profoundly esteemed. Try not to stand excessively near others, and be aware of your non-verbal communication and conduct in broad daylight spaces.

15. **Be aware of garbage:** Japan is an exceptionally perfect nation, and there are not many public garbage bins. Make certain to convey a little sack with you to gather your rubbish, and discard it appropriately whenever you have an open door.

16. **Consider a Japan Rail Pass:** On the off chance that you intend to travel broadly all through Japan, consider buying a Japan Rail Pass. This pass permits you to go on most trains operated by Japan Rail routes, including the popular shinkansen (short train), and can save you a lot of cash.

17. **Visit natural aquifers:** Japan is known for its underground aquifers, or onsen, which offer an unwinding and restoring experience. Make certain to follow legitimate behavior while visiting an onsen, including washing completely before entering the heated water.

18. **Know about the smoking society:** Smoking is as yet normal in Japan, and numerous cafés and bars permit smoking inside. On the off chance that you are sensitive to tobacco

smoke, make certain to search for non-smoking foundations or inquire as to whether there is a smoking segment.

19. **Remove your shoes inside:** As referenced prior, it is standard to take off your shoes while entering somebody's home, and numerous conventional ryokans (hotels) and different facilities likewise expect visitors to take off their shoes inside.

20. **Have a receptive outlook**: At long last, make sure to keep a receptive outlook and embrace the extraordinary encounters and culture that Japan brings to the table. You might experience a few traditions or practices that are new or not quite the same as what you're utilized to, however moving toward them with interest and regard can prompt a more extravagant and more significant travel insight.

Made in the USA
Monee, IL
11 March 2023

29637638R00122